M000235309

RESCUED
FROM
DESTRUCTION

The Story of my journey through the valley of the shadow of death...

Faith A. Oyedepo

RESCUED FROM DESTRUCTION

Copyright © 2005 by:

Faith A. Oyedepo

ISBN 978-2905-30-5

4th Print: March 2007

Published in Nigeria by:

DOMINION PUBLISHING HOUSE

All rights reserved.

No portion of this book may be used

without the written permission of the

 publisher, with the exception of brief

excerpts in magazines, articles, reviews, etc.

For further information or permission, contact:

DOMINION PUBLISHING HOUSE

Faith Tabernacle, Km 10, Idiroko Road,

Canaan Land, Ota.

Tel: 01-7747546, 7747547, 7747548.

Website: www.davidoyedepoministries.org

All Scriptures are from the King James Version of the Bible, except otherwise stated.

Contents

DEDICATION

**This book is dedicated to all those
who stood in the gap for and with
me, and to all those who will, by
my testimony, experience rescue
from destruction.**

INTRODUCTION

The thief cometh not, but for to steal, and to kill,
and to destroy: I am come that they might have life,
and that they might have it more abundantly.

John 10: 10.

One of the cardinal missions of the devil is destruction – he is out to steal, kill and ultimately destroy. What does he want to destroy? Your peace, joy, health, family, job, fulfillment, prosperity, success, and all of those valuable things in your life, especially the ones that cannot be bought with money.

But the good news is that although the devil is out to destroy, Jesus is out to give life and that, in abundance. However, what you don't know, you pay for, just as was the case of Job, who thought that the misfortune he was experiencing was the handiwork of God, and so, in ignorance, he said,

Naked came I out of my mother's womb, and naked
shall I return thither: the Lord gave, and the Lord
hath taken away; blessed be the name of the Lord.

Job 1:21

But that is not God at all! He is not the author of calamity, He does not devise mischief against His people, and He does not use sickness or disease to teach them a

5

lesson. Why? He is not the enemy of man! God is too faithful to fail; He is dependable; He is reliable, and He is more than enough.

That is why when the enemy attacked my body, I knew beyond a shadow of a doubt that although he had come in like a flood, with the intention to destroy, the Spirit of the Lord was available to lift up a standard against him. And Hallelujah, He did!

When the enemy shall come in like a flood, the Spirit of the LORD shall lift up a standard against him.
                                                     Isaiah 59:19b

I came head to head with death, sometimes practically seeing the angel of death at my door, waiting to carry out his evil mission, but death lost the battle over my life. Against the wish of the enemy, now I am actively alive - completely rescued from the clutches of the enemy, to declare the glory of God!

I practically passed through the valley of the shadow of death. The situation was so bad that many people thought it was over with me, but God silenced all my mockers; He turned the table against my adversary; He completely rescued me from the clutches of hell and of the devil, and He can do that also for you, because He is no respecter of persons.

No matter what your present situation is, it is not beyond what God can handle. There is no closed case with God! He opened my grave and liberated me; He can do the same for you, so, don't give up. Remember, He is too faithful to fail - He is dependable and He is more than enough. Praise God!

The summary of my testimony today is **Psalm 118:17:** *"I shall not die, but live, and declare the works of the LORD!"*

The Armor Of Testimony

The Bible says we should put on the whole armor of God. It is important to note that one of the most powerful weapons with which to silence the uproar of the enemy is the word of our testimony. That is why Revelation 12:11 says,

> *And they overcame him by the blood of the Lamb, and by the word of their testimony; and they loved not their lives unto the death.*

Nothing overcomes the enemy faster than the word of your testimony.

David overcame Goliath by the power of testimonies (I Sam. 17: 34-37). He knew he could not have killed a lion and a bear by his physical strength at his age. Since it was God that gave him the victory then, he believed He could, again, give him the head of the giant. So, he went against Goliath, confident that God never fails.

Most testimonies are reproductions of other testimonies. They are pointers to your heritage, showing you what is available to you in God and how you can access the same by standing correctly in the covenant.

Hezekiah was sick unto death at a time during his reign. Isaiah the prophet was sent to inform him that he would die. So the death of Hezekiah was ratified in heaven. He, however, prayed earnestly from his heart, holding on to his testimony of commitment to the things of God, reminding God of how he had walked before Him with a perfect heart. As he wept sore, God heard his prayer and added fifteen more years to him (Isa. 38:1-6).

Testimonies will lead to the rejoicing of your heart, because they authenticate the reality of God. The Psalmist said,

Thy testimonies have I taken as an heritage for ever: for they are the rejoicing of my heart.
—Psalm119: 111

Maybe you have been troubled because things have not been working the way you planned, then you remembered how God did it for somebody else and you begin to rejoice, and in your rejoicing, God steps in to deliver your own into your hands because the Bible says: *Therefore with joy shall ye draw water out of the wells of salvation (Isa. 12:3).* That is how it works, and I see it work for you.

Testimonies help you to generate faith and destroy doubts. In other words, every time you hear a testimony, your faith jacks up! You are stirred up in your spirit to believe that God is still at work in your case. Just as it was with David, your faith rises up and enables you to run towards the Goliaths of life, with the determination of bringing their heads down because, God who did it before is able to do it again.

Testimonies also help to fortify your confidence in God, so that you are able to approach the throne of grace with boldness (Heb.4:16). Hezekiah put God to remembrance (Isa. 38: 3) and he was justified; God had to send Isaiah back to cancel what He had earlier said.

Put me in remembrance: let us plead together: declare thou, that thou mayest be justified.
Isaiah 43:26

No matter what you are facing today, I want to assure you that armed with my testimony, you can go to God and commit Him to do the same thing for you. Because He is not a respecter of persons, the victory He wrought in my life, He will also reproduce in your own life.

Affliction is not from God

3 John, verse 2:

> *Beloved, I wish above all things that thou mayest prosper and be in health, even as thy soul prospereth.*

During that time, I knew right within me, beyond every element of doubt, that that situation, crisis, predicament, ordeal, and affliction in my life was not from God, but had come from the devil to destroy.

In John 10:10, Jesus said,

> *...I am come that they might have life, and that they might have it more abundantly.*

'Might,' in this context, simply means that abundant life is available, but God will not force you to take it; it is available but not compulsory. You have a choice to make, if abundant life is your desire. You can have it if you want - I did, because I chose to!

So the mind has a part to play. If, for any reason, I had accepted in my mind, or thought that that affliction came from God, I know so well, I would never have come out of it.

The scripture says:

> *Who redeemeth thy life from destruction; who crowneth thee with lovingkindness and tender mercies.*
>
> Psalm103: 4.

Whatever situation you might be going through right now, no matter how tough it may seem, I would like you to know it so well and remember it very, very clearly, that God is not the author of it. If He redeemed you from destruction, He won't bring destruction.

James 5:13, says:

Is any among you afflicted? let him pray. Is any merry? let him sing psalms.

He says if anyone is afflicted, such a one should come to God in prayer. If affliction comes from God, God will not be asking us to pray to Him concerning such affliction at the same time. He is not the author of confusion.

It is very important to understand that God is not the author of crisis or affliction. No! But the truth is, in the midst of it all, God can turn it around for your good, taking advantage of the plan and intention of the devil. No wonder the Word of God says, in Romans 8: 28,

And we know that all things work together for good to them that love God, to them who are the called according to his purpose.

So, no matter the situation you might be in right now, God can still make all things work together for your good, and so shall it be for you in Jesus' name. Amen!

Remember the importance of knowledge: Hosea

chapter 4 and verse 6 says,

> *My people are destroyed for lack of knowledge: because thou hast rejected knowledge, I will also reject thee, that thou shalt be no priest to me: seeing thou hast forgotten the law of thy God, I will also forget thy children.*

Lack of true knowledge destroys! So, to be free from destruction, knowledge is a must. Therefore, no matter what the enemy might be telling you right now in that tough time or crisis in your life, never accept the lies of the devil. Never, ever accept that that crisis came from God. No! No! No! God is not the author of it. God is committed to your comfort; He is out to help you, not to hurt you.

This book is, therefore, a testimony of the faithfulness of God, and a guide for all those facing life-threatening situations or crises in life. My prayer is that in case you are going through one affliction or the other, you will find help in the steps God enabled me to take and that you will courageously take the same steps towards your own rescue!

So, come along with me with an open heart, as we travel through this life-transforming material. Remember, the God that we serve is too faithful to fail, He is dependable, and He is more than enough!

Enjoy the journey!

I HAD ALWAYS BEEN

HEALTHY

3 John 2 is a summary of God's intention concerning man:

Beloved, I wish above all things that thou mayest prosper and be in health, even as thy soul prospereth.

I discovered early in life that God's ultimate wish and desire for all His children is for them to prosper and be in health, and that Jesus came to the world primarily to save man from sin and, secondly, to recover man from the clutches of sickness and diseases.

I also discovered, quite early, that God wants man

healthy and vibrant, Psalms 103:3 attests to that fact: *Who forgiveth all thine iniquities; who healeth all thy diseases;* From this scripture, several years ago, I found out that healing is my birthright. I also discovered that healing and forgiveness go hand in hand and that the price for my healing has been fully paid for by Jesus, as part of the redemptive package. Therefore, sickness and disease is no longer my portion in Christ.

As I researched on the subject of healing and health, I found out that even though healing and health is my birthright, knowledge is required to access it. No wonder the Bible says in Hosea 4:6:

> *My people are destroyed for lack of knowledge: because thou hast rejected knowledge, I will also reject thee, that thou shalt be no priest to me: seeing thou hast forgotten the law of thy God, I will also forget thy children.*

You can only recover what you have discovered.

My Personal Journey

I am generally a busy and active person. I enjoy work and must say that I work very hard – every member of my family, as well as my co-workers, know this. Even those who are around me have to work hard, too, because I detest laziness and idleness. So, hard work has always been a part of me.

I had always enjoyed excellent health, for which I

am thankful to God. Considering all that I went through recently however, I have come to value good health more than ever, and, therefore, appreciate God very much for it. In fact, I have learnt to be more grateful for every blessed day that I am privileged to see and experience now more than ever before.

Medically Fit

Every once in a while, as the need arises, I do some periodic medical check-ups and I have done this over the years. Sometimes, I do a clinical examination of the whole body, weight, blood pressure, pulse, blood count, and all of those general physical check-ups. And to the glory of God, my medical history has always been satisfactory; I had always been medically fit.

I have always sought medical advice over physiological issues that I am not clear about and try to put to work any profitable advice at every point in time. I also ensure that I avoid self-medication.

"But why do you do medical examination?" you may ask, especially when you are not sick. Carefully consider the following:-

Prevention, they say, is better than cure. Regular medical examinations, I believe are a preventive measure. A good knowledge of the state of your body could help you avoid future danger, as well as a breakdown.

Adequate knowledge is very crucial for fighting a good fight of faith. Remember that the scripture says *"My people are destroyed for lack of knowledge (Hos. 4:6)*. You can only fight the good fight of faith when you are adequately armed with knowledge.

Isaiah 41:21 says:

> *Produce your cause, saith the LORD: bring forth your strong reasons, saith the King of Jacob.*

Prayer becomes meaningful when you produce your cause and bring forth your strong reasons before God, the judge of the whole earth, with whom nothing is impossible.

So, a regular medical check-up is vital and important to good health. By so doing, you know you have taken care of that aspect and fulfilled all righteousness, according to scriptures (Matt. 3:15).

Eating Healthily

I am also a firm believer in healthy eating. It is a known fact that you are what you eat. Over the years, I have made it a point of duty to get informed and educated about food and proper nutrition. I have learnt and still keep learning from several sources about proper nutrition and this has always been helpful. So, as much as I could, I had always eaten healthily. As much as possible, I also try to avoid late night food and too much fat.

Generally speaking, I take a lot of vegetables and try to steer clear of eating the same thing all the time. I skin my chicken, limit dairy products, avoid impulsive eating and, of course, I fast at least once in a week because, apart from the spiritual benefits of fasting, it also helps to detoxify the body.

I also enjoy taking fruits on a daily basis, instead of snacks, thereby avoiding the temptation of eating fast foods that seem to be everywhere around the country. And even when I eat the right things, I do so until I feel comfortably full, not stuffed.

For years, I stopped taking bottled drinks, canned drinks, packaged juices and the like. Rather I take fresh or homemade juices, and plenty of water. As a matter of fact, I drink a lot of clean water on a daily basis.

Judges 1:15 says,

> **And she said unto him, Give me a blessing: for thou hast given me a south land; give me also springs of water. And Caleb gave her the upper springs and the nether springs.**

God put water on earth for us to drink! Have you ever noticed that water is the only fluid that gives you satisfaction when you drink it? I believe it is the most satisfying type of drink, so I make it an essential part of my meal.

Exercise Plan

But refuse profane and old wives' fables, and exercise thyself rather unto godliness. For bodily exercise profiteth little: but godliness is profitable unto all things, having promise of the life that now is, and of that which is to come.

1 Timothy 4:7-8

When this understanding dawned on me several years back, I began to exercise regularly, primarily to keep healthy and also, because I believe in the law of movement – internal movement, as well as external movement.

By internal movement I mean the movement of food in the internal organs, that is, ensuring that whatever I eat is not allowed to overstay inside before it comes out. To make this possible, I drink a lot of water, knowing fully well that it aids digestion. Also, I take lots of fruits and vegetables.

By external movement, I mean physical exercise. Generally speaking, walking on the treadmill has been my main exercise for a long time and I really love and enjoy it. I have my own personal treadmill that I use, apart from other exercise equipment that we have at home, which I also use quite regularly to keep the law of motion in place. Hallelujah!

Weight Loss

Food, exercise and weight loss are all closely related to health. Some years back, I decided to lose some weight in order to live healthier and generally be freer to move about to be able to carry out my God-given assignment. So, I put the principles I have shared with you in this chapter into practice and lost a significant amount of weight and my weight has been kept smart since then. It has been quite some years now, and to the glory of God, I have managed to keep that weight off!

The Place Of Rest

Even though I am a hard worker, I believe very strongly in the place of rest in taking care of the body. That is why, in spite of my tight schedule as a woman, wife and mother, both in manning the home, as well as keeping up with my official assignments, I try to obey the law of rest, which was instituted by God.

I discovered several years back that God created the heaven and earth in six days and on the seventh day, He rested. Genesis 2:2:

> *And on the seventh day God ended his work which he had made; and he rested on the seventh day from all his work which he had made.*

So, God rested! Even Jesus, our perfect example constantly separated Himself from the crowd after attending to their needs. It is essential, therefore, for man to observe resting periods.

What was the rest pattern? You may ask. Really, the ability to successfully manage yourself with your time, I believe is the foundation to a good rest pattern. Generally, I plan my day ahead of time, so as to enable me do what I need to do at the right time. This helps me to reduce stress. Sometimes, I break my day into two, by setting aside time to rest. It may just be a few minutes of quietness in the afternoon, not necessarily to sleep, but to allow my mind to just relax.

As much as possible, I do not make my home a mobile office. I ensure that I do not transfer the pressure of the office home. At other times, I relax and listen to music in a quiet environment. As much as possible, I do not rob my body of a good night sleep. So, I try to practically balance my activities with adequate rest.

Consequently, with all of these in place, I honestly believed that I was in the best possible state of health, when from nowhere, the enemy attacked my body; it came suddenly, like an ill-wind that blows no good. One minute I was hale and hearty, the next...?

The breakdown wasn't a situation of a gradual deterioration on my health. Only eternity can tell how I successfully went through these great challenges, but one thing I am confident about is that the faithfulness of God saw me through. That is why these words have become my slogan: *God is too faithful to fail, He is dependable and He is more than enough!*

HOW IT ALL BEGAN

In the year 2004, my husband and I had so much going for us: three of our children were in college, while our youngest daughter was still in high school. The children were getting older, so, I had more time for the Ministry than ever before - more time to carry out my official assignments and minister to people. So, we had many plans for the future.

The new ministry jet just arrived and there were many mission outreaches within and outside the country lined up for the year. These mission outreaches were to take place in the course of the year and then, culminate in the annual gathering of the Winners' family World Wide, an event popularly known as "Shiloh," which holds each year in December at Canaan land, Ota-Nigeria, the International headquarters of the Ministry.

Also, my husband was going to be 50 in September that year, and the children and I were looking forward to and planning a big bash to commemorate the occasion. This we thought necessary, especially considering how much he has been a blessing and a role model to the family – and this we had been planning for, for quite a while.

But while we were busy making good plans, the devil was busy devising evil, as his name is. Little did I know that before the year would run out, I would be engaged in the greatest battle of my life. Meanwhile, as a family, we had begun taking steps and fulfilling God's agenda for us for the year.

Precisely, between the last week of June and the first week of July 2004, my husband and I, in the company of some other ministers in our Ministry took off on the first mission outreach for the year within the country, and, of course, we were aboard the new ministry aircraft. On this particular trip, we were scheduled to cover about five cities within the nation, namely Kaduna, Jos, Kano, Abuja and Ilorin – all in different states.

The first few nights on this first mission trip were excitingly memorable. The expectations of the people were so high; you could literally feel God in those meetings. So much was going on that one would imagine that literally everyone who heard about the programme was in attendance – there was also no small preparation made among the team of Pastors, as they received us at the airport, drove us to our hotel rooms and took extremely good care of us.

Then came evening times when we entered into each jam-packed church auditorium amidst excited, joyful shouts of praise unto God; it was electrifying, to say the least.

In each of the stations, numerous souls were saved, diverse healings took place, amazing testimonies were shared and people were tremendously blessed. It could only have been God! It was awesome! God indeed visited his people in an undeniable manner. Every lover of good was excited and lifted.

Then a Pain ...

It was in the midst of all these that the devil violently attacked my body! I know fully well that it was a deadly attack intended for complete destruction, but Hallelujah! Jesus, as usual and as always, triumphed gloriously.

On one of the nights, I slept and woke up the next

morning with a pain on my left shoulder. I thought it was just an ordinary pain, but because I had learnt not to take things for granted, I anointed it and tried to ignore it, but it persisted. So, I decided to mention it to my husband, who immediately prayed for me. I then called one of the ministers' wives in one of the stations to massage the shoulder for me with a balm and she did.

Surprisingly, rather than the pain subsiding, or the shoulder getting better, the pain increased and got worse by the day. Being that we were on a mission trip, I did not want to cause any form of distraction for my husband so, I kept bearing the pain.

By the time we got to the last station, on the last night, during the evening service, the pain became so intense that everything I had on suddenly became so heavy on me; in fact I had to remove my wrist watch in the course of the service. I could hardly sleep that night. I again prayed about it, kept anointing it and managing it, waiting for the trip to be over.

When the trip was finally over and we were on our way back home in the aircraft, I drew my husband's attention to it and again, he immediately prayed for me.

Spiritual Steps

By the time we retuned, the pain had become so

unbearable. I was so restless in my body that when my husband saw the way I was, he knew a spiritual battle was on and he immediately began to wage spiritual war against the kingdom of darkness. He took authority over the enemy and his hosts, lifting up a standard against the works of the devil in my body (Isa. 59:19b).

He prayed heartily, intensely in the Spirit and in his understanding and laid his hands on me, declaring prophetically that the plans of the devil were averted over my health. He then anointed me with oil, decreeing that the battle was over and that victory was ours.

Remember that the Word of the Lord in Romans 8:6 says: *For to be carnally minded is death; but to be spiritually minded is life and peace.* I strongly believe that this foundation that was laid at the onset of this terrible attack must have contributed, in no small measure, to the victory that God eventually gave to me concerning this situation.

I want to say here that when you are faced with a difficult situation in life, do not seek God only after all other means have failed. Rather, consult God first; make him number one! You cannot make God last and expect to succeed. Remember that the scripture says that the arm of flesh will fail (Jer. 17:5-6). No battle in life can ever be too difficult for God to handle. With him, all things – including your own thing, are possible.

He is the Lord of host. Psalms 46:11 says: ***The Lord of hosts is with us; the God of Jacob is our refuge.*** When you give God the first place in every battle of your life, he goes ahead of you and you can be sure of victory at the end of it all. God, who gave me victory, will also do the same thing for you. He is no respecter of persons. Amen!

Medical Attention

Having taken control in the spirit, my husband and I agreed to call a medical doctor, who immediately administered a pain reliever. This was on a Saturday night; I was expecting that the pain reliever would help in, at least, relieving the pain, pending the time when necessary medical examinations would be carried out on the following Monday.

Surprisingly, I began to notice some sudden and rapid changes in my body. A strange kind of radiating pain began first, from my shoulder. It immediately began to spread from the shoulder to the neck, then to the back, and from my back to the left side of the body and, subsequently, to other parts of body. As if that was not enough, my body became numb.

At this point, my husband immediately made arrangements for another set of medical professionals to examine me, refusing to take chances. By this time, I could no longer contain the pain; it was actually piercing through every part of my body. I could neither sit nor stand, so I began to pace up and down the house and then the yard; violently taking authority over the enemy and declaring my total liberty in Christ. I began to pray in the Spirit, as well as in my understanding.

I suddenly remembered how that over the years, I had been taught about the power of the tongue. Admittedly, it is not easy to speak positive words in times of crisis, but I have come to understand that it is the only way out. So, against all odds, I kept boldly declaring God's Word. I became very aggressive about it, knowing fully well that it was a matter of life and death.

I remembered what the scripture says in Proverbs 18:21: ***"Death and life are in the power of the tongue: and they that love it shall eat the fruit thereof."*** So, I began to do what the above scripture says.

It is extremely important to learn to speak positive words, especially in times of challenges. You must watch what you say. You must understand that your expressions ultimately determine your experiences in life. Words are likened to seeds. When you speak them, you sow them. When you sow them, they will certainly bring forth fruits. The kind of fruit you desire should, therefore, determine the kind of words you speak.

However, you do not have to even wait until you get into a life-threatening situation before you learn to speak positive words into your life, as well as that of those around you. Learn to mix your words with God's Word and God will certainly watch over it to perform it. This should actually be a part of your daily life. I can guarantee you, it works!

Just at the point of the sudden changes in my body, the two different sets of doctors arrived. Thank God for these doctors! They were extremely helpful all through. They arrived just at the right time. When they saw my condition, it was very obvious that action could not be deferred untill the following Monday, as initially thought.

They were surprised at my situation, wondering what could have been the cause, especially since I left for the journey in an extremely healthy condition, coupled with the fact that there was no accident or anything of such that could have caused the sudden excruciating pain. They immediately ordered preliminary tests to be done that same night.

Because of the terrible pains, x-rays of different parts of the body were also done – all that same night. While the tests were being conducted, I kept violently and boldly declaring my freedom and total liberty in Christ. However, this inexplainable pain was getting more and more unbearable.

At the end of all the tests, I was given some medications for malaria, typhoid fever, as well as some pain relievers; but the real cause of the excruciating pain was not yet identified. Meanwhile, the x-rays were sent to a specialist for reading.

It was difficult to actually understand what was happening at this point, because the doctors had no clue as to the cause of the sudden, excruciating, inexplainable and unbearable pain. It was, indeed, a deadly attack from the pit of hell. There was no accident, no falling down - nothing before the trip commenced or in the cause of the trip that could be said to be the root-cause of the attack. However, I knew that even if no one else had an idea about what was going on, God before whom all things lay bare, knew exactly where this attack came from, and I was persuaded, He was in absolute control.

As time went on, in addition to all the preliminary tests, more comprehensive and extensive medical examinations were carried out; just to be sure that no stone was left unturned and, of course, to fulfill all righteousness. Tests, such as ECG and fasting blood sugar were conducted; my blood pressure, as well as cholesterol level were examined, and several others. I also had some more x-rays done. The results were all satisfactory.

I Examined My Heart

One very important step I took at this crucial time was to examine my heart. I decided to do this, primarily, to ensure that my personal relationship with God, as my Savior, as well as my Lord, was intact.

I gave my heart to God and got born again many years ago as a teenager, and have always treasured my relationship with Christ, above any other thing in life. I never wanted anything to come between me and my God.

Early in life, I made a covenant with God that nothing would ever be able to separate me from Him or from loving Him, as long as I live (Rom.8:35).

Also, in 1976, I covenanted to make Jesus Lord of my life. I decided that He shall forever be Lord of all in my life. I wanted to examine my heart to be sure that this was still in place and that my heart was right and at peace with God. So, I did and was satisfied.

Secondly, I had to examine my heart to be sure that my relationship with people was also peaceful and acceptable to God. I had always valued people, as well as profitable relationships, knowing fully well that man was created to connect. I ensured that, in my heart, there was no such thing as bitterness, unforgiveness, hatred, malice, strife, deceit, and the like (Heb. 12:15, Eph.4:32).

This became necessary because, I knew that such things could easily open the door to the enemy. Strife and envying, for instance, can create a conducive environment for every manner of evil work (James 3:16).

I was aware of the fact that these are issues that I had to personally search out, confront and handle. They are issues that no one else can handle for another. Life, my husband says, is a product of personal responsibility. Having done this, to the best of my knowledge, I was satisfied. I then knew that my victory in this situation was guaranteed.

One thing I knew for sure was that as long as I am a child of God, my victory is guaranteed in every situation of life.

1 John 5:4 says,

> *...for whatsoever is born of God overcometh the world; and this is the victory that overcometh the world even our faith.*

This means that whosoever is born of God has a heritage of victory with him, no matter the contrary situation that you may be seeing before you! On the other hand if you are not born of God, you are likely to remain a victim of the wickedness and cruelty that is prevalent in this world, just as 1 John 5:19 says:

> *And we know that we are of God, and the whole world lieth in wickedness.*

So, to everyone that is born of God, you are saved from the cruelty and wickedness that is in this world – for truly, the whole world lieth in wickedness!

You are saved to become a winner. You are not saved to suffer defeat, shame and reproach. You are saved to command victory and shine forth as a star. Whatever situation you might be facing right now, no matter how tough it may seem, as long as you hold on to Jesus, your victory is sure. God who gave me victory when men thought it was all over in my life, will do the same thing for you!

That was why I knew from the onset that the devil's terrible attack on my life, with the intention of out-right destruction, was not going to end in defeat for me, but would be turned into a testimony; and glory to God, it did. So, from the beginning, I knew that my victory was already guaranteed. I was too sure, just too sure! I knew God is too faithful to fail! He is dependable! and He is more than enough!

This was the beginning of a battle that progressively became more intense and lasted for almost one year. But at the end of it all, we are, today, celebrating the triumph of Jesus – which shall be forever! Halleluyah.

3

COMBATING INITIAL

SYMPTOMS

At this time, excruciating pain became a seemingly permanent situation. The pain was inexplainable! It was throbbing and piercing through every part of the body. It was persistent, sparing no part of the body at all. I had never experienced such before. It was unbearable!

Consequently, several other symptoms began to appear. To get a good night sleep became an uphill task. I battled with insomnia. To lie down on any part of my body was so difficult. If I tried sleeping on the right side, I felt pain. If I turned to the left, I encountered pain. I could neither sleep on my back nor on my tummy without experiencing terrible, excruciating, throbbing and piercing pain all over the body.

I, then, began to appreciate much more than ever before, the ability to sleep as a gift from God. No wonder the scripture says in Psalm 127:2 that *... he giveth his beloved sleep.*

Think about it for a moment! That you are able to sleep and wake up is a gift from God to you. Never assume it or take God for granted any more concerning this. Many there are that live in big houses with great possessions, but lack good sleep. Good sleep is a gift from God. Even though there is medication that makes you sleep, there is none to make you wake up! Several people have taken such medication to sleep and never woken up.

This must be why the Psalmist said:

I laid me down and slept; I awaked; for the LORD sustained me.

Psalm 3:5

From henceforth, each day you wake up, express your gratitude to God for giving you the privilege to see another day. You wake up each day because God has being sustaining you. Refuse to take God for granted, so you do not get grounded in life!

One moment, I would be feeling terribly cold inside out and shivering; the next moment, I would be feeling terribly hot and be sweating profusely. It was a terribly strange experience.

As time went on, I gradually began to lose appetite and every time I attempted to eat, whatever I ate, I threw up. With this, I began to experience general terrible body weakness. I lacked the required energy to do just about anything, as I constantly felt tired and exhausted. Each time I summoned energy to attempt any minuscule task, I immediately became dizzy. The medication I was given for treating the fever and the pain did not seem to help; rather, it seemed to worsen the situation, perhaps because they had their own side effects.

As time went on, rather than the situation getting better, it was actually getting worse. Gradually, things I could do before now seemed so difficult.

But as these symptoms went on and on, one thing I thank God for, is the privilege to have known the Lord Jesus Christ as my Saviour early in life as a teenager. That early encounter with the Lord also opened me up to the Word of God at a very tender age. Therefore, I had been privileged to be fed by the Word for several years, and had developed a culture of taking time each day to swallow God's Word as raw as it is presented in scriptures. The word of God had become my way of life. This Word-foundation was crucial in building me up spiritually.

My husband said, sometime ago, that training is what leads to triumph; therefore, if you are not trained in the Word, you are not ready for triumph, no matter how long you have been saved!

God's Word as Medicine

I began to take the word of God as medicine. My husband and I began to stand on scriptures on a daily basis. Every blessed day, he would read some scriptures to me or give me some to read; at other times he would have somebody read those scriptures to me. We knew that standing on the Word of God, which is the incorruptible seed, is a sure guarantee of victory any day!

Also, I noticed that each morning, I woke up with at least one definite scripture given to me personally by God. I would then read those scriptures or have someone read them to me. Thus, I kept standing on scriptures throughout the time of this attack. Such scriptures as,

Psalm 107:20 - *"He sent his word, and healed them, and delivered them from their destructions."*

Psalm 118:17 - *"I shall not die, but live, and declare the works of the Lord."*

Isaiah 59:19b - *"When the enemy shall come in like a flood, the Spirit of the Lord shall lift up a standard against him."*

Exodus 23:25 - *"And ye shall serve the Lord your God, and he shall bless thy bread, and thy water; and I will take sickness away from the midst of thee."*

Deuteronomy 7:15 - *"And the Lord will take away from thee all sickness, and will put none of the evil diseases of Egypt, which thou knowest, upon thee, but will lay them upon all them that hate thee."*

Psalm 34:10 *"The young lions do lack, and suffer hunger: but they that seek the Lord shall not want any good thing."*

Isaiah 54:17 *"No weapon that is formed against thee shall prosper; and every tongue that shall rise against thee in judgment thou shalt condemn. This is the heritage of the servants of the Lord, and their righteousness is of me, saith the Lord."*

3John 2 *"Beloved, I wish above all things that thou mayest prosper and be in health, even as thy soul prospereth."*

Day by day, as these scriptures were being unfolded, I began to write them down and declare them. I kept warring a good warfare with them, knowing that God is too faithful to fail, He is dependable and He is more than enough!

Please understand that victory in life answers to faith and faith answers to the word of God; so, if victory is your desire, the word of God must be your focus! There-fore, every time you are confronted with a challenge in life, engage in a search for the right Word from the scriptures.

The Bible says, in Job 6: 25: *How forcible are right words!* ... So, right words have the required force to force your adversaries to bow, no matter how many and how bent they are on destroying you. And all your enemies will bow in Jesus name!

Psalm 107:20 also says: *He sent his word, and healed them, and delivered them from their destructions.* That is why the man to be pitied is the Word-lazy Christian, because he remains a cheap victim of defeat.

Standing Strong in Prayer

Is any among you afflicted? Let him pray. ...

James 5:13

So, not only did we stand strong in the Word, we paid attention to the force of prayer. My husband, close friends and family members prayed consistently, ceaselessly, tirelessly, and on a daily basis for me. Our spiritual parents and mentors in the ministry prayed fervently, as well. In actual fact, the first breakthrough I had with sleeping was as a result of the prayer our spiritual father and mentor in the faith, Pastor E. A. Adeboye prayed for me.

Prior to this time, as I said before, I had found it difficult to sleep. But then, came this night when after speaking with me on phone, Pastor Adeboye prayed for me and gave me some specific spiritual instructions on what to do. I obeyed those instructions and for the first time, in a long time, I was able to sleep. Truly, prayer changes things!

Let me tell you this, it is very crucial to have some people in your life, particularly spiritual parents with higher grace, unction and anointing, that can speak into your life and destiny in times of challenges. My husband and I learnt this early in life and it has always brought us tremendous blessings. It will help you too.

Think of it: who speaks into your life in times of difficulty? You need to wisely and prayerfully locate someone, if there is no one yet, and do it now – for your own good and safety!

However, I did not only rely on the prayers of others, I was also praying for myself, standing upon the authenticity of scriptures and relying on the integrity of God not to fail. And sure enough, God did not fail me! He will not fail you either. You can count on him!

Standing Strong in Fellowship

They go from strength to strength, every one of them in Zion appeareth before God.

Psalm 84:7

Over the years, I had come to understand and value the importance of fellowship. So, in spite of the indescribable pain, the neck collar I was wearing, the general body weakness and all the other symptoms, as much as I could, I took part in most of the church services.

The scripture says:

But upon mount Zion shall be deliverance, and there shall be holiness; and the house of Jacob shall possess their possessions.

Obadiah v. 17.

During some of such services, I would be so tired and weak that getting out of my seat was a major challenge. But then, I kept on combating all these symptoms by faith, believing that in Zion lay strength for the weak. I also went ahead and got many tapes of such services, as well some that I could not attend and watched them many times over. I kept receiving spiritual strength from all these.

Let me say here that in times of difficulty, the best place to be is Zion – church and fellowship! Admittedly, the natural man would want to withdraw from fellowship at such times. But really, this is the time to be addicted to fellowship more than ever. So, do not withdraw from church when the going gets tough; it is actually the only true solution centre (Heb. 10:25). Rather than run away from church, therefore, run to church!

A Decision Of Faith

By faith, my husband and I agreed that the remaining planned mission trips for the year both within and outside the country should continue.

It was evident, and we understood it clearly, that it was the plan of the devil to frustrate the will of God concerning the success of those trips, so we concluded that even if I was not going to be able to accompany him, he should go ahead, so that the work of the ministry would not suffer. With the situation on ground at that time, this was a tough decision to make. This was purely a decision of faith! And God honored it.

However, we were in touch all the time. Wherever he traveled within and outside the country, we were in touch on a daily basis. He consistently prayed for me and read scriptures to me or gave me scriptures to read every blessed day! Oh! Thank God for a godly husband. He actually gave me a covering throughout this period. Only God can reward him for such efforts on my life, and He sure will.

As he went on those mission trips, most people never knew of the situation we were facing at that point in time. In actual fact, it was much later that many of the Pastors in the stations and the countries where he went, got to know.

Many could not imagine nor understand how my

husband was able to cope with such trips and, at the same time handle the challenge of this deadly attack of the devil on my life. But God sustained and strengthened him to go through it successfully.

Amazingly, all those mission trips were awesomely successful, to say the least! Many souls got saved and there were diverse testimonies to the glory of God. God did honor His Word. Only He could have done that, and to Him alone be all the glory!

Winning The Battle Of The Mind

I have come to find out that truly, the mind of man is the battlefield of his life. Really, where your life goes is determined to a great extent by where your mind goes. A great man of God once said, "Blind minds are worse than blind eyes." This is very true. If only the mind can be enlightened, then, victory is sure.

With all these symptoms on and no seemingly significant medical help, the enemy began to attack my mind. There was a fierce battle ragging in my mind. Oh, it was severe, but God is faithful!

2 Corinthians 4:4 says,

> *In whom the god of this world hath blinded the minds of them which believe not, lest the light of the glorious gospel of Christ, who is the image of God, should shine unto them.*

Nighttime Became Nightmare!

All kinds of negative thoughts and imaginations began to bombard my mind. Sometimes, when it was time to go to bed at night, the enemy would say, "Will you ever sleep through the night?"; "Will you ever wake up without pain again?'; "What if you cannot sleep tonight?; "What if you slept and never woke up?" "What if you have just a few more days to live?" "Now that there is no medically known cause for your situation; what if there is no known medical help or solution?"; "Will you ever be healthy again?" What if you could never live a normal life again?" "What if, and what if?" The 'what ifs' never seemed to end!

You know, the Bible calls the devil the prince of the power of the air (Eph. 2:2). Nighttime rather, than being a time of good sleep, suddenly became my nightmare!

Emotional chaos gripped my mind, as all kinds of thoughts were coming to attack it. But thank God for His Word! Each time the devil attacked my mind, I audibly replied him with the Word of God. Remember that the scripture says that the stranger shall fade away out of their hiding places when they hear your voice! (Ps. 18:44-45).

One major lesson that I learnt during this period of attacks on my mind was that, the best way to fight negative thoughts was not with positive thoughts, but first and foremost with positive words. Secondly, you fight them with positive thoughts. You never win the battle by fighting negative thoughts with positive thoughts only. You must open your mouth, speak positive words against those negative thoughts and then, you can now, subsequently, begin to fight those thoughts that are negative with both positive words and thoughts.

The Bible says, in Psalms 81:10:

> *I am the LORD thy God, which brought thee out of the land of Egypt: open thy mouth wide and I will fill it.*

So, each time I got those 'what if' thoughts, I opened my mouth to shut the enemy up with those scriptures, upon which I was and am still standing. Please understand that you can only possess what you proclaim! (Mk. 11:23)

Some of those scriptures are the ones quoted just a while ago and more of them I will be sharing with you and listing out in the course of this writing. It was a long and tough battle, but to the glory of God, he gave me victory at the end of it all!

The only person permitted to give up on any battle of life is a dead man! But as long as you are alive, you must be strong and fight to the finish.   So refuse to give up!

1 Samuel 4:9 says,

> *... quit yourselves like men, and fight.*

Are you facing a particular difficulty in life right now to which there seems to be no end or solution? Be reminded that the devil is a liar! Stand fast in Christ. With God on your side, you shall surely make it. For, if God be for you no one and no difficulty of life can successfully be against you (Rom. 8:31).

Then 1 Corinthians 16:13 says,

> *Watch ye, stand fast in the faith, quit you like men, be strong.*

As you stand strong in the Word, you will surely win every battle of life, including the battle of the mind! He did it for me; He will do the same for you as well.

ALL HELL BREAKS LOOSE!

Things came to a head months later, when, during service on a Sunday morning in church, I was to lead the congregation in worshipping God with our offerings. Suddenly, as I walked towards the altar, I noticed some strange feelings all over my body.

I got to the altar, picked up the microphone and was about to speak when suddenly my whole body became terribly weak. My two hands became so weak and before I knew it, I could no longer hold anything and both hands just went straight down – both of them dropped to my side. As soon as that happened, the microphone dropped from my hand onto the podium.

Instantly, my face changed. I became somehow

temporarily unconscious. I couldn't really explain it, but all I knew was that I couldn't understand what was going on any more. I didn't know where I was and so I stood there speechless, right on the altar.

People waited to hear me speak, but I was just standing right there, speechless. However, miraculously, I was still on my feet, but speechless nevertheless. It felt like though some invisible forces held my feet firmly on the ground and prevented me from falling. This, I believe could only have been God.

Many people from afar didn't really know what was going on, being that the auditorium is a very large one; seating conveniently over 50,000 (fifty-thousand) people. All they saw was that I was standing there speechless.

However, some who were close by and observant, sitting not too far away from the altar, probably had an idea that something strange was definitely going on. Instantly, some people began to pray, calling the name of Jesus, pleading the blood of Jesus; and then, two of the senior pastors and my husband came over to meet me there on the altar.

Miraculously, all in a moment, as I stood there wordless, God came on the scene; I regained consciousness and instantly, strength came into me as my husband and those two pastors stood there with me and I was still able to minister that day. I even walked back to my seat all by myself and sat in the service throughout that day. Truly, God is a very present help in times of need! (Ps. 46:1)

As I stood tongue-tied, one amazing thing that I noticed was that right in my heart, there was no fear of any kind. My heart was intact; my confidence in God and in His omnipotence and faithfulness were unwavering. My physical condition notwithstanding, I knew that the faithfulness of God was more than enough to see me through that challenging situation and it did!

That was the beginning of another era. All hell was just about to break loose!

Worsening Physical Conditions

After this incident, I began having some strange experiences. Shock waves began radiating all over my body. This happened repeatedly and each time, I got physically weaker and weaker. It became a frequent occurrence. It was usually a frustrating experience, to say the least!

As time went on, things that I could easily do before, became far-fetched. For instance, to carry or even read my Bible became an uphill task; walking also became a serious issue. To sit down was difficult; standing up was a challenge. Several times, my husband would support me by holding my hand while we walked into church, just to give me the physical support that I needed to be able to cope with that indescribable challenge.

With time, I was even unable to carry out personal hygiene for myself. I needed assistance and support to get virtually everything done, including toileting! Things began to change so rapidly. Conditions began to worsen so terribly; nighttime became scary, because it was usually a serious battle time.

To find sleep was a serious task, and even when I got sleep, I was always fighting one battle or the other in my sleep. Several times, I would wake up from my sleep to find myself pleading the blood or calling the name of Jesus Christ.

Several times in church, when I sat down, I became so weak that I couldn't stand up without support. As things progressed, physical changes also began to take place in my body. My eyes got affected; I could hardly read any more. Different parts of my body such as the legs, hands and other parts of the body swelled up. The neck became stiff and every attempt to turn it resulted into terrible crisis. Also, one of my hands from the shoulder downwards became stiff. It was a terrifying experience.

Some other medical professionals were contacted. More medical examinations and tests were conducted. The result? Really, nothing significant, except that one of the results of those tests queried "tendinitis". The controversial question was that even if this was so, could it have resulted into this kind of sudden and inexplainable crisis, having seemingly unbelievable symptoms?

All the medical professionals and experts handling my case were surprised, as there were no acceptable medical explanations to what could be the root cause of all these alarmingly strange symptoms. One common question that most of them kept asking was whether there was any sort of accident; because it was difficult to trace or explain the root cause of these symptoms: but there was no accident of any kind!

On different occasions, two of them said there are many people who have worst cases than what the result of my test queried and are going about their daily duties without being aware. However, as expected, more medications were prescribed to treat the symptoms. But this did not seem to help, but rather worsened it.

One of the professors handling my case asked in despair one day: "What are we really treating?" Much later, after God rescued me, about three of them confessed that all along, they knew that it was a completely spiritual case that required divine intervention and not medical treatment.

At this point in time, something amazingly strange began to happen. There was this mysterious, ugly, black, devilish structure that stood continuously at the entrance of the door to the room where I was. This ugly creature was boldly labeled, "death angel," and persistently stood at the entrance of any room I was in for months and I could see it every day – apparently, I was the only one who could see it.

Change Of Environment

It is a known fact that a positive change of environment enhances health. Therefore, after serious considerations, my husband and I decided that a change of location might be necessary for me. We reasoned that the change in location would provide an excellent opportunity for me first, to be better focused and be able to more seriously apply myself to spiritual principles. Secondly, it will provide an avenue for me to take proper rest, avoid stress, refresh and take good care of myself.

Thirdly, we also felt that traveling would make for better spiritual concentration on the mission trips that my husband was divinely mandated to fulfill. Then of course, fourthly, I would also have the opportunity for better medical attention. And lastly, in that anonymous environment, I would also be able to avoid distractions from unending visits, which are characteristic of the African people.

So, We Traveled

The night we were traveling out, my husband and I were driving out of our home, prophetically named *"Light House,"* when the devil whispered to me, "This journey shall be a journey of no return" and immediately, the Spirit of God within me reacted violently, and inspired me to reply the devil's threat with a song of victory:

"He has promised He will never fail,

I will hold on Him, I will hold on Him,

He has promised, He will never fail,

His faithfulness is forevermore,

His faithfulness is forevermore.

God has promised me He will never fail,

I will honour Him, and I will follow Him,

My God has promised He will never fail me,

So His faithfulness is forevermore,

His faithfulness is forevermore".

So in reaction, I continued to sing. Everyone in the car heard me singing, not knowing the battle that was going on in my mind.

We went on the long international trip; it was definitely a challenging journey, but thank God I arrived alive and well. On the trip, I battled tirelessly with all the aforementioned symptoms, including difficulty in catching my breath. My legs got so swollen on the trip, that I had to expand the shoes I had on by cutting the upper part open.

Upon arrival, the health care professionals that attended to me could not hide their astonishment as to how I made that trip. But to the glory of God, I did! One of them later said it could only have been a miracle that I made the trip alive. According to him, many normal people in that condition would have become unconscious, to say the least.

As soon as we arrived, my husband prayed for me, anointed me with oil, and laid hands on me. He also spent some time with me before returning back to Nigeria. Some great men of God also came to pray for me. Naturally, with my limbs as terribly swollen as they were, my movement was so retarded that I needed help, even to get in and out of bed.

Further Examinations

Thank God for hospitals, medicines, doctors, modern medical equipments and know-how, but in the course of this challenge I came to understand that while physicians may do their best to treat you; it is God that actually heals. Deliverance and rescue comes only from God!

I must also add that one cannot help but be thankful for Christian medical practitioners, who have faith and confidence in the healing power of the Almighty God; they surround you with an atmosphere of faith that encourages you to keep pressing on, trusting God to perfect that which He has started!

So, I went in for further medical tests and examinations. This time, it was very exhaustive and thorough. The existing chronic symptoms raised several questions, as to what could be the cause. Could it be a problem with the neck? I met with specialists in this area and had my neck examined. Relevant tests were carried out, including MRI of the neck. The result showed that my neck was normal.

Could it be arthritis? I met with a rheumatologist who carried out several tests as well. I had about five different blood works done, searching for arthritis. I had x-rays of the various joints done, including the ankles, knees and waist. The result of all the tests showed that all was normal and no trace of arthritis at all.

Considering the symptoms, could it be a nervous breakdown? I met with a consultant in this area and had several relevant tests done. Even, I had EMG and nerve conduction velocities of the upper extremities done. It proved that all was normal. Could it be a problem with the brain? Related tests and examinations were conducted, including MRI of the brain. The result showed that my brain was in perfect shape.

To show you just how thoroughly I was examined, I had MRI of the spine, CT Scan of the cervical spine and others as well. Every imaginable test was carried out: you name it, I had it! All these produced normal results indicating that I was in perfect shape. The MRI of the shoulder was also done.

My respiration was tested; my blood pressure and my pulse were taken again and were declared normal. My skin was checked, and the conclusion was that it was tested negative for rash. My lymph nodes were checked and were found normal, my chest was checked and said to be clear. My nose and mouth were examined as well. The examination was exhaustive, to say the least!

I was in the hospital for over one week, not for treatment, but just running all these tests. My lab works were sent to various hospitals and specialists for readings. This was to be expected, so as to know the course of treatment to administer, considering the prevailing symptoms. They tried their best to see if they could find some key with which to help. Oh, they were all extremely helpful! Only God can reward their efforts. God bless them all!

I met with several consultants and specialists. The

conclusion of one of the specialists was and I quote: "I'm not exactly sure what is causing her problem here." Medical science had reached its limit! But thank God that you and I have a supernatural God that can make a way where there is no way! With Him, there is no impossible or closed case. To him we can always appeal.

Finally, the coordinating specialist made it clear that it was important and necessary to look up to God, with whom all things are possible, for a final solution, he being a very vibrant Christian. Having fulfilled all righteousness, therefore, we put our faith in God for a complete and total deliverance.

At this point, it became abundantly clear that this situation was not an issue of a sickness or disease that required healing, but was an outright attack of the devil from the pit of hell. It was also clear that the devil's intention was definitely to destroy and that only God could rescue me. And He did! It was a satanic conspiracy from hell against my life, but God squashed and destroyed it completely. Halleluyah!

However, for the frozen shoulder that was identified, a procedure was employed to break it loose while therapies and exercises were recommended to help with restoring motion. Thereafter, we kept our gaze absolutely and solely on Jesus, as the solution provider out of that predicament (1Cor.10:13).

We believe in miracles and have seen countless miracles happen in many places as well as in our own ministry – even to the point of seeing the dead raised back to life, so, it was easy for us to trust God for a miracle of rescue over my life. For sure, we understood that it was a serious attack from the pit of hell, but that the faithfulness of God was going to prevail. Our faith was intact and truly, at the end of it all, God prevailed triumphantly and gloriously!

Wow! God is too faithful to fail! He did not fail me and he sure will not fail you. Remember, I am just like any other person, except that my total trust was in Him. God is no respecter of persons. So, you can depend on Him.

Handling Malicious Publications

It was a field day for what my husband described as "irresponsible journalism." Many News agencies sought to publish any bit of information they could lay their hands on – whether there was any truth in the allegation or not.

It seemed that they were just out to make quick money by taking advantage of the challenges I was going through. One cannot but wonder who their alleged sources were, but at every phase of the challenge, journalists published whatever their imaginations could capture.

Some of them alleged that the challenge was a stroke, occasioned by some bad news, others even published that I was having complications in pregnancy; yet, some others were quoted as saying they heard from some authoritative source that I was paralyzed on both legs, etc.

There was all manner of falsehood, with no substance to it whatsoever and malicious publications pushed sensationalism to the limit! One such journal published that I was dead. Several times close family members and staff received phone calls from journalists hinting at or otherwise trying to confirm the supposed news of my death. But glory to God in the highest, I am alive and well, to prove to the world that, indeed, those publications were nothing but the ranting of hell!

Halleluyah, I am still here! Because Jesus lives, I shall live also!

As the Bible says, which became true in my situation: *The kings of the earth set themselves, and the rulers take counsel together, against the LORD, and against his anointed, saying, Let us break their bands asunder, and cast away their cords from us* (Ps. 2:2-3).

But my God, ... *disappointeth the devices of the crafty, so that their hands cannot perform their enterprise* (Job 5:12)!

God, who did mine can, and will surely do yours too! So, no matter your situation, I can boldly say that

there is no closed case with God, including your own!
Praise God!

TAKING MY DELIVERANCE

BY FORCE

And from the days of John the Baptist until now the kingdom of heaven suffereth violence, and the violent take it by force.

Matthew 11:12

Until you become violent in the spirit, you cannot take what belongs to you. You have to come to a point where you accept responsibility over the challenges you are facing and do what it takes spiritually to overcome. Life is all about responsibility; and as my husband says, if you are not ready to accept responsibility, you may likely die a liability.

As an individual, I got to a point where it became very clear to me that, support from all others notwithstanding, I had to accept personal responsibility for my deliverance. My soul had to come on the scene violently then. The devil came to destroy, but I told God that I chose to live and not die, so that I could declare His works.

There and then, I knew what to do! I decided to remind God that my being alive, rather than my death was going to be a testimony and, therefore, beneficial to the promotion of His Kingdom. I also reminded God that my husband, children, local church and the body of Christ at large, as well as He (God) needed me alive.

The symptoms notwithstanding, I made up my mind to accept responsibility, so as not to become a liability. I, therefore, took practical, radical steps to enforce my deliverance. I located the manifold wisdom of God and violently applied it to my situation, so as to teach principalities and power a lesson.

> *To the intent that now unto the principalities and powers in heavenly places might be known by the church the manifold wisdom of God.*
> Ephesians 3:10

I want you to follow very closely as I share some of

these radical steps with you here. I guarantee you out-standing results, if you take these steps during your day-to-day living. These are both defensive and offensive in nature, so you do not have to wait until a time of difficulty or crisis in life before you begin using them. They are failure-proof!

The Word of God

The first radical step I had to take was the Word-step. I began to consciously feed my spirit man with the Word of God at every point in time. God's Word became my life and only source of hope. I knew within me, beyond every iota of doubt that, persistent and discouraging symptoms notwithstanding, God cannot lie and His Word works. My confidence in God's Word was intact.

The Bible says, in Proverbs 4:20-22:

> *My son, attend to my words; incline thine ear unto my sayings. Let them not depart from thine eyes; keep them in the midst of thine heart.*
>
> *For they are life unto those that find them, and health to all their flesh.*

I began to attend to God's word!

My son bought me a walkman, a Bible on Cassette, as well as healing-related teachings of anointed men of God. So, I began to listen and devour them like a hungry person every blessed day. I had my walkman in my ears day and night; when I went to bed, I had it on until I slept; I woke up with it and every available moment, I was loading my heart with the Word. I just saw it as an opportunity to feed my spirit man with the Word of God. In addition, I kept confessing the Word of God day and night, as I listened to it.

Whatever situation you might be going through, you must remember that what you feed your spirit man with plays an important role in determining how fast your deliverance comes. So, watch what you hear and what you listen to; it has a lot to do with your deliverance becoming a reality.

As often as I could, I made time to watch the services at Faith Tabernacle, Canaan Land, Ota-Africa on the Internet, thus, staying connected to the word of faith that I was sure would result in my liberation.

The Name Of Jesus

One of the radical steps I took at this time was to constantly arm myself with the failure-proof weapon of the name of Jesus.

The scripture says:

> *The name of the LORD is a strong tower: the righteous runneth into it, and is safe.*
>
> Proverbs 18:10

God has provided a shelter, a strong tower, a wall of defense for the believer: it is the name. There is safety in the name of Jesus! The name of Jesus is the security of the saints.

To enjoy the security in the name, however, the believer has a personal responsibility to run into it. How do you run into the name for safety? You may ask. Simply by calling on it in faith! So, during this time, I constantly called on the name of Jesus. I remember several times I would go to my closet, bathroom or some quiet place and just call J-E-S-U-S! Oh, what a place of safety! The good news is that there is no overdose of it. You can call the name as often and as many times as is needed.

The Bible says:

> ... *and his name shall be called Wonderful,* ...
>
> Isaiah 9:6

The name of Jesus is full of wonders. It worked wonders in my life, especially at that very critical moment. It is only what you call that answers to you, so, times without number, I called on the name of Jesus with the violence of faith for rescue.

Truly, there is victory, power and wonder in Jesus name! The power in that name is failure-proof. There were times when the situation became so unbearable that the immediate thing I could do was to scream that name. And praise God, there were always instantaneous answers from the throne.

David overcame Goliath with the name! (I Sam. 17:45-50). What is that Goliath that is harassing your life and destiny? The name of Jesus will settle the issue! "Could it be that simple?" You may ask. The Bible talks about the simplicity of the gospel. The name worked for David and he overcame Goliath; it worked for me and rescued me from the clutches of the devil, so I know and I am confident it will work for you too!

The Communion

Over the years, I had come to understand the importance of the communion table with relation to health, vitality, longevity and deliverance. There is wonderworking power in the communion!

In 1 Corinthians 10: 16, the Bible says:

> *The cup of blessing which we bless, is it not the communion of the blood of Christ? The bread which we break, is it not the communion of the body of Christ?*

The communion represents the flesh and the blood of Jesus Christ. And when we partake of this, we are empowered to live like Jesus. During His ministry on the earth, every attempt of the devil and his agents to destroy Him failed. So, I knew that as I partake of the communion, every attempt of the devil over my life and destiny would also fail.

With this understanding, I began to partake of the communion table several times a day before every meal – breakfast, lunch and dinner. Whenever either my husband or any of my children were around, I always had them bless the communion and serve me, especially when I was so weak and I couldn't do this by myself. When I was alone, I tried to do it for myself and even up till now, I partake of the communion regularly. I believe that the communion is a rescuing weapon that cannot be overcome by the enemy.

It is one of the end-time, many-sided wisdom of God for turning the table against the enemy in the lives of His children. It brought me deliverance, and I guarantee that it will secure deliverance and blessing for you also. Amen!

1 Corinthians, chapter 11 and verse 30 says:

For this cause many are weak and sickly among you, and many sleep.

It became clear to me also, that if those who partook of the communion table unworthily became weak, sickly and died; if I partook of it worthily, in faith, discerning the Lord's body, then I would receive strength, overcome sickness and be rescued from the clutches of death.

And really it worked, thank God!

I see it work for you, enforcing your deliverance and helping you obtain your expected result!

The Anointing Oil

I am a strong believer in the efficacy of the anointing oil as part of the mysterious, manifold wisdom of God.

Isaiah, chapter 59 and verse 19, says:

> **So shall they fear the name of the LORD from the west, and his glory from the rising of the sun. When the enemy shall come in like a flood, the Spirit of the LORD shall lift up a standard against him.**

From insight, I believe that the anointing oil is the Spirit of God mysteriously package in a bottle and designed to communicate the power of God to your body. It is also one of the standards God raises to stop the floods of life from overwhelming His children – and there is no enemy that can humiliate the standard of God. The anointing oil is God's power and standard handed over to the believer to completely disgrace the enemy and send him packing from our vicinity!

It was with this understanding I had about the anointing oil that I began applying it daily, more so during the challenge I constantly anointed myself, the bed and my room where I slept; even the door beside which the ugly *death angel* stood was consistently anointed!

The symptoms, notwithstanding, I kept on applying this mystery on a daily basis. I am aware that the anointing oil, the yoke destroyer was one of the weapons that destroyed the intended activities of this evil, death angel!

I can honestly say that it was via the administration of the anointing oil, that I practically experienced the intervention of the Holy Spirit in my situation and total deliverance, which is evidenced in my life today.

> **And they went out, and preached that men should repent. And they cast out many devils, and anointed with oil many that were sick, and healed them.**
>
> Mark 6:12-13

Also, James 5:14 says,

> **Is any sick among you? let him call for the elders of the church; and let them pray over him, anointing him with oil in the name of the Lord.**

The anointing oil of a truth is a yoke destroyer! It is a burden lifter! It destroyed the yoke of the enemy over my life and destiny. God is no respecter of persons; what He did for me, He will do for anybody else, if you will take time to also apply this manifold wisdom of God in faith!

The Blood of Sprinkling

And they overcame him by the blood of the Lamb, and by the word of their testimony; and they loved not their lives unto the death.

Revelations 12:11.

The blood of Jesus Christ, when sprinkled, incapacitates the activities of the destroyer, just as was the case when the death angel struck in Egypt. Remember that as many as had the blood smeared on their lintel and doorposts were preserved from the destructive mission of the angel.

With this in mind, I constantly sprinkled the blood of Jesus all over the room, the house where I was, and over myself.

Hebrews 11: 28 says,

Through faith he kept the passover, and the sprinkling of blood, lest he that destroyed the firstborn should touch them.

I tapped into the virtue in the blood of Jesus, by faith and it worked for me. I am aware that the blood of sprinkling was instrumental in the destruction of the death angel that consistently stood at the door of my room then! The blood incapacitated it and sent it packing! Wow! There is awesome power in the precious blood of Jesus Christ!

The Mantle

> *And besought him that they might only touch the*
> *hem of his garment: and as many as touched were*
> *made perfectly whole.*
>
> Matthew 14: 36.

A mantle is simply a blessed piece of clothing material from a prophet, which then, carries the unction of the prophet. It can also be used to communicate the power of God, as was the case during the earthly ministry of Jesus, resulting in great signs and wonders (Matt. 9: 20-21).

Paul was also greatly used of God in this area. Special miracles, signs and wonders took place in his ministry via the application of the power cloth, the mantle.

Acts 19: 11-12 says:

> *And God wrought special miracles by the hands of*
> *Paul: So that from his body were brought unto the sick*
> *handkerchiefs or aprons, and the diseases departed*
> *from them, and the evil spirits went out of them.*

Even today, God still performs special miracles by the hands of living Pauls and Peters. During that period of challenge, the mantle joined the list of arsenals that I leveled against the kingdom of darkness. I had a mantle blessed and sent to me by our spiritual father. The mantle, when applied in faith can work wonders!

Feet Washing

After that he poureth water into a bason, and began to wash the disciples' feet, and to wipe them with the towel wherewith he was girded.

Peter saith unto him, Thou shalt never wash my feet.

Jesus answered him, If I wash thee not, thou hast no part with me.

John 13:5-8

Jesus, Himself, instituted the mystery of feet washing. While He was here on earth, He washed the disciples' feet in order to deliver their part in him to them. Ever since God revealed this to my husband, I had, in faith, partaken of the mystery of the feet washing.

I had no doubts that this mystery is one of the secrets by which God delivers the portion of the saints to them. So, during the period of challenge in my life, every so often, I had my feet washed to take possession of my portion in Christ, which includes deliverance. My portion of rescue was delivered to me; you can lay hold on yours, too!

The Prayer of Faith

Affliction can be cheaply destroyed by the instrumentality of prayer. So, one way to effect healing in the physical is by praying the prayer of faith:

74

Is any among you afflicted? let him pray. Is any merry? let him sing psalms.

And the prayer of faith shall save the sick, and the Lord shall raise him up; and if he have committed sins, they shall be forgiven him.

James 5:13&15.

However, much more than praying for myself, I began to pray for other people that needed divine intervention in different areas of their lives. I remembered, at this point in time that whatever I made happen for others, God will make happen for me.

Also, the case of Job in Job 42:10 came to my remembrance;

And the LORD turned the captivity of Job, when he prayed for his friends: also the LORD gave Job twice as much as he had before.

James 5:14 and 16 commands us to pray one for another to effect healing. So, I began to invest in praying for other people. Difficult as it was, I began to take my eyes away from my own personal needs and to invest passionately in praying for the blessings and deliverance of others.

I also had times of prayer walk, where I would walk around the house, with the energy I had, or pace up and down the passageway, praying in my understanding, as well as in the spirit for myself and for others who needed God's intervention. It was not easy, but it pays!

Truly, we serve a God that answers prayers. And just as He answered mine, He will answer yours, as well!

Sacrificial Giving

Sacrificial giving has always been a part of my husbans's and my life as a couple – whether financial or material seed, at different times, we have given sacrificially unto God. So, again, during this period in my life, my husband and I gave sacrificially to God for my total deliverance.

Sacrificial giving is a biblical principle. Carefully, look at this scripture and see what it says about the subject of sacrificial giving:

> *And the king said unto Araunah, Nay; but I will surely buy it of thee at a price: neither will I offer burnt offerings unto the Lord my God of that which doth cost me nothing. So David bought the threshing-floor and the oxen for fifty shekels of silver.*
>
> 2 Samuel 24:24

I remember clearly, one day I began to hear "all of gold", "all of gold", "all of gold." This is in line with the Word of God in Exodus chapter 35 and verse 5, which says:

> *Take ye from among you an offering unto the LORD:*

whosoever is of a willing heart, let him bring it, an offering of the LORD; gold, and silver, and brass.

In verse 29, the children of Israel obeyed this command, and willingly gave God their best!

The children of Israel brought a willing offering unto the LORD, every man and woman, whose heart made them willing to bring for all manner of work, which the LORD had commanded to be made by the hand of Moses.

I knew God was the one speaking to me, because I had heard Him in this fashion in time past. So, in obedience to His Word, I joyfully, excitedly and willingly gathered all my gold jewelry, every bit of it and gave them sacrificially unto God, and then I had peace in my heart. Although this was not the first time I was doing this, this time, again, I knew that God had accepted my sacrifice.

In addition to this offering of gold, we gave several other items, including vehicles and other valuables to God. We knew that, in line with Psalms126: 5, God would not fail us! My husband also vowed unto God that at my return, he was going to give certain sacrificial seeds unto God, and this he did upon my arrival.

And just as God stayed the plague when King David offered sacrificially unto God, He did the same thing in my life and stayed the hand of the destroyer. Oh, sacrificial giving works! It is one of the end-time mysteries to disappoint the tokens of the wicked. It worked and is still working for me; it will work for you too!

Please understand that God is never in need! It is man that is always in need. The scripture says that the earth and all its fullness belong to God (Ps. 241). Whatever you give to God came from him in the first instance. Therefore, my giving and your giving of offering never add to God, rather, they add to us. Will God wear gold? Definitely not, but it is my life that needed to wear a new look! And now, that new look is evident.

Someone might say, but what do I have to give? Listen to the voice of God and be led by him!

A Joyful Disposition

Therefore with joy shall ye draw water out of the wells of salvation.

Isaiah 12:3.

The Kingdom of God is a Kingdom of wells. Everything that man will ever require in life is available in the wells of salvation. These include deliverance, healing, prosperity, promotion - you name it. Whatsoever man will ever require is available in those wells, but it takes joy to access your blessings.

With this understanding, despite the discouraging symptoms I was experiencing in my body, I chose to remain joyful; I maintained a joyful disposition. To this end, I surrounded myself with joyful people; that way, their joy rubbed off on me and helped me throughout that season of my life. My husband was constantly joyful, making it impossible for depression to have access to me at any time. Whenever my children were around, they also brought up jokes to make us laugh and rejoice. This motivated and encouraged me a lot. Those jokes were like a "spiritual massage" bringing healing to me, both internally and externally. Truly, a merry heart doeth good like a medicine (Prov. 22: 17)!

What joy does is to help diffuse tension; it deflates pressure and helps you enjoy a stress-free atmosphere at all times. Let me give you a piece of advice: be careful about the kind of people that come around you when you are facing a tough time. Remember, two cannot walk together except they be agreed (Amos 3:3). If you surround yourself with negative people, who are only there to sympathize with you, you will have nothing to show but aches and pains at the end of the day.

Admittedly, it is not easy to maintain a joyful disposition when pain is ravaging your body and all hope seems to be lost. But it is not sympathy you need; it is results, and the surest way to get at them is by a joyful disposition and a merry heart! Give it a trial in your life, you will not be disappointed.

Gratitude Attitude

Another potent tool, which I employed to work out my salvation during this period, was a gratitude attitude. It is natural to be irritable at such a time as this, but this robs you of the blessings of God. Your being irritable might even drive helpers farther away from you, thereby, driving you into isolation, which destroys faster than anything else.

I took a strong decision to be more grateful, both to God and to man during this season of my life. Each time I woke up, opened my eyes and saw another day, irrespective of the symptoms and pains I was experiencing, I constantly lifted up my voice to give thanks unto God for the privilege of another day; for the privilege to live. I refused to take God for granted so that I would not be grounded!

In the same vein, I began to consciously show gratitude to the people around me that offered assistance in one way or another, by my attitude. I concluded that all those who were helping to get things done, to ensure my physical comfort, such as my children, relations, brothers and sisters in the faith, medical practitioners, neighbours and everyone that was used of God to assist me in one way or another, deserved to be appreciated.

I saw whatever assistance they were able to render, as a privilege and not a right and as much as I could, I verbally expressed my appreciation for their input and support. This helped me a great deal in building my attitude, as well as my character.

Well, all of the above, among many others, were the manifold wisdom of God I put to work to enforce my deliverance. They were the things I had to do to take my deliverance by force.

As I conclude this chapter, it is important to let you know that I did all the above with absolute faith and confidence in God. Remember that the Bible says:

> *...the just shall live by his faith.*
>
> Habakkuk 2:4.

So, I took a decision and had to deliberately ensure the presence of faith in my heart as I took all those steps. Faith in the heart is required, if those weapons must deliver your desires.

The steps discussed in this chapter are both defensive and offensive in nature, so you do not have to wait until you are faced with a life-threatening situation before you apply them. And what's more, there is no overdose on any of them; you can put them to work as needed! It works!

I must say here, that, this is by no means, a comprehensive list of the things I did. However, I believe that as you put these to work in faith, your desired liberty, freedom, deliverance, rescue and blessings will also become a practical reality in your own life, in Jesus' name. Amen!

6

I WAS NOT ALONE

...But woe to him that is alone when he falleth; for he hath not another to help him up.

Ecclesiastes 4:10b

Nobody can successfully live life in a vacuum; we all need each other! Sometimes we need people to help us get to where we are going, other times we may just need a helping hand, a warm embrace, or someone who is just there to pray for us and encourage us. I was a beneficiary of help at a time in my life when I needed it most. During that time, help was available in terms of prayer by several people: they not only prayed and interceded fervently for me; they stayed close by and helped me in innumerable ways.

Prayers of the Saints

During this period, as I mentioned before, several people prayed for me. Many of them had never even known us personally, many of them we had never met face to face; but especially due to the malicious publications that were being circulated at this point in time, many people everywhere began to pray for my deliverance. Groups of people, as well as individuals organized prayer meetings and ceaselessly prayed. Oh! Thank God, because He answers prayers!

Acts 12:5 says:

Peter therefore was kept in prison: but prayer was made without ceasing of the church unto God for him.

While Peter was kept in prison, the Church made prayer unto God for him without ceasing and Halleluyah, Peter was miraculously rescued. This was exactly my own story. The saints of God prayed in unity, in oneness, even though in different locations (there is no barrier in the world of the spirit), God heard and He wrought deliverance. The same way He did it for Peter, He opened my grave, the iron chains broke in pieces, the stone was rolled away and miraculously, I was rescued!

Oh how God honoured and answered the prayers of the saints! Never under estimate the power of prayer. It is one of the most potent forces of the saints. People in different nations, who were aware, prayed fervently, and God heard and answered.

For everyone who was a part of this rescue prayer team, whether individually or as groups of people, God saw you and your investment. I may not have been there to see you, I probably may never get a chance to ever meet you physically to be able to thank you, but remember, God who saw your prayers in secret, will definitely reward you and in your own time of need, men from far and near will also rise up on your behalf to pray for your rescue, in the name of Jesus Christ. You have sown good seeds into your own future; no devil will rob you of your benefits.

Enjoying Dividends of Divine Connections

It is extremely important to have someone who is spiritually above you to speak into your life in times of spiritual battles. Don't fight your battles alone; there are certain spiritual battles that you certainly will not be able to handle by yourself all alone. You need to be connected to those who are spiritually above you. Such individuals with higher unction and greater grace manifest upon their lives and ministry, who can speak into your life in times of crisis. No matter your level in life, there are and will always be people who are above you, spiritually. All you need is spiritual insight to locate them.

My husband and I discovered the importance of spiritual parents many years ago, and ever since, we have ensured a solid and unbroken connection with spiritual parents. During this time of crisis, my husband and I were constantly in touch with our spiritual father in the faith and mentor, in the person of Pastor E. A. Adeboye, and his wife. They stood strong in prayers on my behalf.

I remember one early morning Mama Adeboye drove all the way to our home, with a bowl of very delicious soup, which she had prepared all by herself. She came not only to drop the bowl of soup, but also to spend time praying, interceding, supplicating, and standing in the gap.

Pastor Adeboye, on his part, blessed a mantle and handed it over to me, using it as a point of contact for my complete deliverance and recovery from every intention of the wicked one. They not only stood openly by us, they were also there for us. They were always in touch, constantly giving counsel and every time I had an opportunity to speak with either of them on the telephone, they always prayed and spoke words of deliverance into my life. Oh, thank God for spiritual parents who are always there for you. Today, God has given us the victory and I believe that our victory is also their victory.

That is why I strongly believe that you also need such men in your life. Refuse to join the company of prodigal sons. Remember, you will always need a spiritual father. Get back to your roots in case you do not have one, locate a spiritual parent in the faith with higher unction, so you can enjoy the many graces of God upon their lives at one time or another in this journey of life.

Dr. T. L. Osborn's Prophetic Visit

One day, Dr. T. L. Osborn, a man greatly used of God in this generation, walked into the room where I was, knelt down and prayed fervently for me. That prayer was extremely timely; it marked a turning point in my life. On another occasion, he came visiting in the home where I was. As soon as he entered, he looked at me straight in the eyes and said: "They wanted you dead, but you fooled all of them". Then he pointed his finger at me and declared, "But you shall not die but live and declare the works of God."

Then he sat down, shared a few other things with me and knelt down again, held my hand and prayed passionately, decreeing my total liberty. When he stood up, he told me a very remarkable story that I can never forget.

He said that one day, the devil was standing with

two of his demons, but while he was busy here and there, those two demons came close and were attempting to enter our home. Dr. Osborn said, "But this house is the house of God, the devil can never have access to it!" So, when the devil lifted up his eyes and saw those two demons attempting to enter our house, he quickly called them back and asked them what they were looking for and said: "Don't enter that house. Don't enter that house; come back here now." And the devil called his two demons back to order.

But, again, while the devil was looking here and there, those same demons attempted the second time to enter into our home. Just then, the devil lifted up his eyes and saw those two demons making a second attempt into our home and once more, the devil called them back and then gave them a strong warning, never to attempt entering our home anymore in their life, this time explaining that if they knew what, he, the devil suffered during his own futile attempts, they would not be so foolish as to make the same mistake!

And Dr. Osborn smiled, turned back and said, "This house is the house of God, no devil can ever enter this house." With that, he said goodbye and left. That dramatic story that Dr. T.L. Osborn related that day was very prophetic. It was a mysterious parable that had come to pass practically. Every attempt of the enemy failed in my life!

Oh, how we as Christian today need to get connected to spiritual parents from whom we can draw inspiration and strength in times of need. These spiritual parents stand in the gap for us in times of challenges.

My husband and I have taken this provision seriously over the years and we have benefited severally from such relationships. I know and I'm sure that such relationships will also be beneficial to you.

Take a close look at what the scripture says concerning this here:

> **And without all contradiction the less is blessed of the better.**
>
> Hebrews 7:7

You are the one to benefit! May the Lord give you understanding.

Other Prayer Support

Many other great men of God: some, heads of their own various ministries, others, pastors and leaders within our entire ministry network, all rendered intense prayer throughout this season for us. Many of them paid visits to our home physically and were a blessing to us in no small measure. Some of them came several times to pray in our home or organized prayer sessions in their own ministries or stations for me. I remember one of such great men of faith came several times, prayed and encouraged that I violently look away from the prevalent symptoms because my total liberty was sure. To all of such, I shall be eternally grateful.

I specifically remember one time when some of the leaders within our ministry network came to our home. They organized days of prayer and fasting for me, standing strong in the gap, crying out to God to show up in my favour and rescue me from the grip of the enemy. Also, some individuals, families and groups organized prayer sessions, just for me. Oh, I felt loved and encouraged! God Almighty, the true rewarder, will surely reward every one of you.

Helpers of My Joy

All through this trying period, I always had people with me and around me, serving one purpose or another. At different times, they were always there: to read to me or help write down some scriptures, attend to my meals, go for prayer walks with me, attend to several other personal needs and ensure my general comfort (Col. 4:11).

These all left the comfort of their homes to be around me during that period, just to ensure that everything was alright. Some of them are wives of some leaders within our ministry network, within and outside

Nigeria, some are wives of leaders of other ministries, some are family relations, others include co-workers, neighbors and well-wishers; they were all helpers of my joy (2 Cor. 1:24).

To all such people, and many more that are too numerous to mention, my prayer is that they will not miss heaven's abundant rewards, in Jesus' name. Amen!

FAMILY SUPPORT

No matter how much support one receives from friends and well-wishers during a time of crisis, one of the greatest supports is family support. When a husband stays by his wife and parents stand by their children, or vice versa, the challenged party will beat almost any odds.

The great greek philosopher, Socrates, always encouraged his students to marry. He was said to have told them humorously that if they marry good wives, they will live long happy lives, but if they marry bad wives they will become philosophers! Anyway, his philosophy was that marriage makes you live happier and longer.

That is why I cannot play down on the great support

I received from members of my family – both nuclear and extended. In fact, the extended family members on both sides were of great assistance. But most importantly, my husband and children helped me a great deal.

At this point, I want to seriously encourage family members, that is, husbands, wives and children, to stay closely knit together as much as possible. This becomes necessary because sooner or later, especially in tough times, each person will require the help of another.

My dear husband and all our wonderful children were there and, indeed, helped me a great deal during this period. Indeed, they provided the needed assistance during this trying period. I am immensely overwhelmed, by their support.

My Husband

Ecclesiastes 4:9 says,

Two are better than one; because they have a good reward for their labour.

I must say that I count it a great privilege to be married to my husband, Dr. David Oyedepo, a man of courage and great boldness in God!

During this period of my life, he kept declaring the end, which is victory, from the beginning. His faith and confidence in the Almighty God was unshakable.

It means a lot to have somebody close to you, who is able to stand in prayer with you through thick and thin. There were several times when, naturally, all hope seemed practically lost, but my husband kept holding on to God, standing with me through it all and declaring the end from the beginning.

Several times he saw my secret tears, especially when no one else was there, but in it all, he refused to give up, boldly and confidently declaring that all shall be well. He kept declaring the Word to me all the time. Several times he would hold me close to himself, kneel down beside the bed and speak faith filled words, such as: "It is well!", "You have overcome!", "You are more than a conqueror!", "The devil has lost the battle over your life!", "You shall make it!", "You shall not die but live and declare the works of God!", "We shall go round and preach the gospel together!", "We will go places for God!" He kept on re-assuring me of the faithfulness of God and the infallibility of his Word. Oh, how I treasured and treasured those invaluable moments!

He spent several long hours seeking the face of God concerning me and searching the Word for answers. And as soon as God showed some thing to him in His word, he would come and share such words with me. Virtually, every blessed day, morning and night, he would read specific scriptures to me. Many times, when we were not in the same city or country, while he traveled out on outreaches, he kept doing the same thing on the phone. No day passed by without him declaring the Word of God to me.

Sometimes he would list out specific scriptures related to any situation I was encountering and give them to me to read. Sometimes he would dictate these scriptures on the phone and ask me to read them. At other times, he would ask whoever was around me at the time to read out those scriptures to me. Truly, two are better than one!

> *How should one chase a thousand, and two put ten thousand to flight, except their Rock had sold them, and the LORD had shut them up?*
>
> Deuteronomy 32:30

There were times when he had to be called upon on emergency to attend to me. Each time, he would pray intensively from his heart asking God to intervene, turn the table against our adversaries and wrought deliverance.

I specifically remember one time, when I was gasping for breathe and pinning away: everything seemed to be coming to a stand still; he had to be sent for on an emergency. He rushed in to the place where I was. I was with our first daughter on this particular occasion, who, on seeing my condition, immediately began praying in the spirit: pacing up and down, shedding tears and crying out to God for mercy. On this particular occasion, naturally, all hope seemed to be lost.

But when my husband was called, he immediately left what he was doing and rushed in to where I was. When he saw my condition, he knelt down beside my bed, held my hands and prayed fervently, asking God to prove Himself in my life. I remember him saying "Lord, prove that you sent me! Lord, prove that you sent me! Lord, prove that you sent me!" And sure enough, He did!

I have written a little love letter here to appreciate my husband for standing by me:

Oh my Darling,

I salute your courage and boldness and unwavering faith in God, as well as your demonstration of love throughout this period. I am overwhelmed by your love. I am short of words. You prayed to God to prove that He sent you and He did.

I want to say to you, as I have said times without number when I came out of this trying time, that I do not know where I would have been today if I was not married to you. I would probably have been forgotten, if it were not for your boldness of faith, your absolute confidence in God, your support and your love. God has put you in my life to preserve my destiny. I am greatly indebted to you.

You are an unparalleled man of valor. Surely, the grace of God will keep multiplying upon your life and ministry in new and greater dimensions in Jesus' name. Therefore, I say unto you:

Many men have done valiantly, but thou, my husband, my darling, the husband of my youth, Dr. David Oyedepo, thou exellest them all (Prov. 31: 29).

Only God can reward you. And He, God Almighty, will surely do so. I love you, I love you, and I love you. I am grateful, I am grateful, I am grateful. We shall yet do greater things for God and His kingdom together. Halleluyah!"

There were several times when my faith seemed so weak, but my husband would come and say something humorous or give me something special that would lift up my spirit, fire me up, increase my faith and keep me going.

There were several little, little acts of kindness that I will ever live to remember, such as, having to help me carry out personal hygenic activities and other menial things that practically no one else would want to do for another. I am eternally grateful!

I remember that after God gave us the victory and I started regaining my strength, he would ask me questions such as: "Is there anything I can do for you?",

"Would you need my assistance in this area or that area?", "Would you need me to get this done?" And I would say thank you, telling him, I could now do all these things by myself.

Really, without any doubt, God honored his faith; He saw my husband's practical demonstration of confidence in Him. God did not disappoint us. That same God that you serve will never disappoint you. The God of David Oyedepo is truly the living God. Amen!

Our Children

I practically walked through the valley of the shadow of death (Ps. 23:4), but God worked an undeniable miracle in my life!

The following is a letter I have written to bless our wonderful children for the role they played when I walked through that valley of the shadow of death:

David (Jnr.), Isaac, Love, Joys:

Truly, you all are as arrows in the hands of the Almighty God. He used you in no small measure, as weapons of war on my behalf.

My beloved children, we are proud of you all. Only heaven and eternity has the record of what you have invested into my life. I would like to remind you that the seed of love that you have sown shall never be lost, in the name of Jesus Christ. Amen!

At different times during this period, when naturally, all hope seemed lost, you wrote several letters with encouraging words and spirit-lifting scriptures. (Some of them are included in this work). *They were immensely helpful to me, at a time I needed them most.*

Truly, God used you as arrows to speak with the enemies in the gate. I am proud of you. Together we shall keep proclaiming this everlasting gospel. The devil has lost completely over our lives and destinies. And definitely, affliction shall never rise again the second time.

My precious children, David, Isaac, Love and Joys, you shall excel! You are really the epitome of godly children. My God will preserve your life and destiny. There's a great future ahead of each of you and you shall get there, in Jesus name. I love you! I love you! I love you! I am eternally grateful and indebted to you all. Thank you! Thank you! Thank you! Amen.

With the words in the above letter, I speak blessings over your lives! Those declarations shall be permanent, in Jesus' name.

Psalm 127:3-5 says:

Lo, children are an heritage of the LORD: and the fruit of the womb is his reward.

As arrows are in the hand of a mighty man; so are children of the youth.

Happy is the man that hath his quiver full of them: they shall not be ashamed, but they shall speak with the enemies in the gate.

God blessed our marriage with four wonderful children, two boys and two girls. All of them, throughout this period of challenge, stood so strong with me, reassuring me of God's faithfulness: supporting and lending helping hands every time I required them. They stood in the place of prayer throughout this period, praying individually and together for me. But apart from prayer, many times, it would be one of them who will be present to anoint me, the bed where I slept, or several times, the room and the house where I was.

At other times they would serve me the Holy Communion or sprinkle the blood of Jesus around me. I found out that because they had been brought up in the fear of the Lord, they are knowledgeable of the scriptures and were able to, by faith, administer the various mysteries of the Kingdom for my liberty. Even when it seemed that hope was lost, they kept at it, believing God that He will never fail us, and, thank God, He did not!

Also, whenever they were around, they were always available to render any form of assistance that I needed or required per time. They performed several little acts of kindness that very few people would be willing to do for another. They assisted me, in no small measure, even in carrying out personal hygiene.

Faith-Filled Words

My children were always there speaking or writing faith-filled words to me throughout this period. As I said earlier in the book, several times, when they were around, they would gather around me just to make me happy. They would crack jokes, share experiences, compelling me to laugh and to rejoice. So, together we would laugh, talk and rejoice, just to make me happy; strengthen me, dispel depression and help me take my eyes away from the physical and put my confidence in God. I value all those precious moments and I am eternally grateful to God for them all.

I have taken time to include some of my children's letters to give you an idea of just how deeply they inspired and lifted up my spirit: particularly considering the fact that they were written at the most trying time, when naturally speaking, my situation seemed completely hopeless. There were several others, but these are just some of them. With an open heart, carefully read these along with me!

1. **From our first son:**

January 12, 2005

"THERE ARE NO SETBACKS IN GOD'S PLAN"

Dear Mummy,

Every situation that seems like a setback is only a platform for you to be set forth. Forward movement is the only option for any child of God. Every time the Bible recorded any hindrances, it became the foundation for great miracles. When Jesus fed 5,000 people, the miracle would have been pointless if the need for food was absent. But the hunger of the people created a need, which, in turn, led to one of the greatest miracles in the history of the world.

There is also the story of the woman with the issue of blood. This woman's story would never have made it to the Bible if she did not have that issue of blood. However, what seemed like a set back propelled her into history through her healing. Therefore, approach every negative situation as a platform to be set forth, which, in other words, means every situation is a launching ground into a new level in God.

So, like a great boxer with God as our coach, it is time to knock out the devil. So Mom, I just wanted to encourage you. I love you and I am rejoicing with you for the victory you have received by faith.

I love you, Mom.

— David Jnr.

KNOCKOUT ROUND.

2. **From our second son:**

MOMINSIN,

This is by far the best summer I have ever had in my life. I know that you think you stressed all of us, but it was really a pleasure to see God perfect His healing in your life.

Mummy, words cannot express how much I love you. You are the best thing that ever happened to me. I thank God for your life.

Mummy, I ... really miss you and I cannot wait to come home this summer..

Thank you Ma, for your care and understanding, even when it was difficult for you.... Mummy, I love you for just letting me be me..

I love you Ma with all my heart for being the best mother in the world.

Please take care of yourself and rest, as you go back home.

Thank you.

— Isaac

3. From our first daughter:

DEAR MOM,

I thank God for the miracle He has began in you. I am sure that He will perfect it. You are precious and God will not fail.

I know that God has more in store for you and the devil already lost. This year will be a year of greater grace and favour.

I love you so much Mum and I know that God does not disappoint His people.

You are the best mom and I love you so much. Thank you for everything and may God continue to bless you with the desires of you heart.

Your daughter,

— Love

4. From our second daughter:

January 2005

Scriptures On Healing

MUMMY,

These seven scriptures have become your healing scriptures. At the name of Jesus, every knee must bow. The name of your sickness is not above the name of Jesus

(Matt. 11:28-30). The name of Jesus has healing power and it is able to heal you. God's gentle hand will heal you today and I believe that today is your day of victory.

God loves you and therefore, He will heal you.

1.   *Exodus 15:26*

   When you hearken to the voice of the Lord and obey his commandments, He will not put any of the diseases that he brought on the Egyptians.

2.   *Exodus 23:25*

   When you serve the Lord, He will bless what ever you eat and drink and He will keep sickness away from you.

3.   *Proverbs 4: 20-22*

   The Word of God gives life and HEALTH to those that read and obey it DAILY.

4.   *Proverbs 17:22*

   The Word of God is telling us that being MERRY (Joyful) in your heart gives you good health. Therefore, JOY = HEALTH (Formula).

5.   *Isaiah 40:29*

   God is a good God. He helps those that need his help and he gives strength to those that need it.

6.   *Isaiah 58:8*

The glory of the Lord is the reward for those who have

the fear of the Lord and part of glory includes health, not just health, but extraordinary health.

GOD IS YOUR HEALER MUMMY.

7.   *Revelation 5:12*

> **The Lamb that was slain gave us seven (7) spirits including HEALTH and God's word can't lie so; your healing is sure this night, before you wake up.**

Your healing will come in a flash. Don't let people stop you from getting your testimony. God is no respecter of persons. God's plan for us is for good and not for evil to give us an expected end. GOD LOVES YOU. He gave His Son for you to be saved. This alone, shows that He really loves you. God has not changed so if He could raise Lazarus from the dead, your case is not a different one. He can heal you and He will heal you.

I LOVE YOU MUMMY, BUT GOD LOVES YOU MORE.

TODAY IS YOUR DAY OF HELAING.

God is always on your side.

— Priscilla (Joys)

Despite the discouraging physical conditions and circumstances around me, my children kept on speaking these kind of words of faith, confidence and encouragement. And, Halleluiah, today, it has become a reality! I remember few months ago, after my deliverance, I was in the kitchen cooking, when my first son came up to me and expressed gratitude to God and how amazed he was to see me, once again, doing the things I used to do before. He was overwhelmed. My all wished me well and truly, now it is well.

I am eternally grateful to all of you. Praise God.

8

THEN CAME

A TURNING POINT!

When the Lord turned again the captivity of Zion,
we were like them that dream.
Then was our mouth filled with laughter, and our
tongue with singing: then said they among the
heathen, The Lord hath done great things for them.
The Lord hath done great things for us; whereof we
are glad.
Turn again our captivity, O Lord, as the streams in
the south.
They that sow in tears shall reap in joy.
He that goeth forth and weepeth, bearing precious
seed, shall doubtless come again with rejoicing,

bringing his sheaves with him.

Psalm 126:1-6

In December 2004, when the year 2005 was prophetically declared to be my year of turning point, I strongly desired the manifestation of that prophetic word of God in my life; I believed God and held on to the word, my condition, notwithstanding. I had no idea how God was going to make it happen, considering my situation then; but my heart was fixed, trusting the Lord.

No matter what situation you might be in right now, I would like to let you know, there is no closed case with God!

Ecclesiastes 9:4 says:

For to him that is joined to all the living there is hope: for a living dog is better than a dead lion.

As long as you are joined to Jesus, there is hope for you.

Beating the Odds!

After undergoing a procedure for my shoulder, I had to start exercising it and also, different parts of my body, because at that time, mobility was near zero. I had to start learning how to walk again – in actual fact, my children had to order a walker for me to start practicing and learning how to walk.

Several times, during the day, I would take a hope and confession walk, declaring the word of God and confessing scriptures as I walked around my room and the house, I looked so fragile but at the same time, I refused to sit or lie still.

Then one morning my husband instructed me to read Luke10: 19. He also said that I should ensure that I walk around as often and as far as I could, confessing that scripture as soon as I get out of bed for the next few days.

> *Behold, I give unto you power to tread on serpents*
> *and scorpions, and over all the power of the enemy:*
> *and nothing shall by any means hurt you.*

Luke10: 19

So, in obedience to his instruction, I would get up several times with my walker, and move around, confessing that scripture. Whoever was around would walk round with me, just to ensure that everything was okay. I kept at it for days, confessing, "I am treading upon serpents and scorpions and over all the powers of the enemies and nothing shall by any means hurt me".

Wriggling in pains and terribly uncomfortable, but with absolute confidence and faith in the Word of God that cannot lie, I kept on confessing. I kept at it! I kept at it! I did this for a few days and I think, about the fifth day, after walking around and making this confession, I lay on my bed. My son and one pastor were standing just by the door of the room where I was. My son lifted up his eyes, and suddenly, saw a green snake close to the door of the room. Surprised, he called the attention of the pastor and then proceeded to smash it's head and killed it. Even while the head was already smashed, the body was still shaking for quite a long time. He hit it again and ensured it was completely dead.

Later on, my son called my attention to what had happened and asked me whether I knew the implication. I told him I didn't and then he reminded me about the scripture that I had been quoting and confessing for the past few days. He made me to understand how that it was a sure proof that that scripture had been fulfilled in my life.

This was the beginning of a new chapter in my life. With this experience, I began to beat the odds. God began to turn my captivity.

That was the beginning of my turning point!

Getting Progressively Better

After this incident, I began to notice progressive improvement in my body. Day after day, things began to improve. Then, something else very mysterious happened. In our home in Nigeria - prophetically named 'Light House', a big, black, ugly bird was found completely dead, knocked down by the power of God, right at the entrance to our private sitting room, just before the bedroom! The light of God in the 'Light House' was too much for the devil!

That was a strange thing to happen, especially because no one was in the house and all the windows and doors were locked. By the way, we had never, at any point, in time seen a bird inside that house, but this time around, with no one there, and with all the windows and doors securely shut, this ugly devilish bird found its way in. What was amazing was how it headed directly for our bedroom!

But how it was slain completely by the power of God is still a mystery till today. The dead bird was gathered and burnt to ashes. This was the second physical manifestation of the power of God in action. The enemy thought he had concluded his plans concerning me, but how wrong he was; totally wrong!

Then, mysteriously, the very day when that bird was being burnt, calls started coming in from people asking about my person, fearing that the worst had happened. But praise God, He turned the table against my mockers and turned my captivity around.

Thereafter, I began to notice certain landmark changes.

After the first snake was killed and the bird died and was burnt, I discovered that my strength was gradually returning. In spite of these improvements, I refused to let up the intensity of my spiritual warfare.

I kept on making my confessions everyday, listening to the Word of God daily, and administering the mysteries on my person on a daily basis. As I did all these persistently, strength began returning to me. My circumstances began to change for the better, slowly, but surely. I believe God was watching over His Word to perform it in my life!

And then I noticed that my hope in God began to get fired up. Then, gradually, I was able to read my Bible much more than ever before. I began to have the greatest hunger for the Word of God. Prior to this time, reading my Bible ord any other thing was an uphill task because of indescribable pains and discomfort. So, it was to my greatest delight that I could read the Word of God again and not only that, but to have a great craving for the Word of God, much more than ever before. The more I studied and listened to it and fed my spirit man, the more strength I began to gather.

Another Physical Manifestation

To bring the number of physical manifestations to three, one day in my husband's office, a long, winding, poisonous live snake was found! It was eventually killed. That was also very mysterious, more so because that particular office is on the 2ⁿᵈ floor of the building and the windows are never opened.

Meanwhile, my husband was in that office working the previous day for almost 7 hours in the night, but God kept him against the will of the adversaries. So, it remained a mystery how that kind of snake could get to that floor! We knew that it must have been the work of the devil and his agents. But thanks be unto God, who has given us the victory and made us more than conquerors!

The devil lost the battle and that marked a remarkable turning point in my recovery.

"What is the relationship between these happenings and your condition?" you may ask. Pay very close attention here:

After the snake was killed, the first major change was that the death angel, that dark, ugly, structure that constantly stood at the entrance of my room vanished and disappeared from that day, never to return again.

Oh! Truly, I knew that the burden had been lifted; I knew that my grave was opened. I knew that life had been restored. And from that moment forward, dramatic changes began to take place.

Then gradually, I was able to walk again; my eyes began to function effectively. Prior to that time, I could not see properly anymore, but from that moment forward, my eyesight regained normalcy.

Also, I regained my appetite. Prior to that time, I couldn't eat; I'd lost appetite and was so physically weak that to get out of bed was an uphill task. But after this incident, I regained my appetite and gradually was able to eat, bit by bit. As soon as I began to eat, I began to get stronger and stronger by the day.

Prior to that time, I required assistance to get in and out of bed, but I found out that I could easily get in and out of bed by myself without assistance, from that moment. I began to get better by the day. God proved Himself faithful. What a mighty God we serve!

And then, one morning, I began to hear the voice of God say to me, *"You can do it!"*, *"You can do it!"*, *"You can do it!"* I knew it was God because I know His voice and the way He speaks to me. So, I got off bed, got into the shower and bathed myself for the first time in about nine months! Even though it was extremely difficult and painful, I kept at it! After the shower, I was able to dress myself up, all by myself – again, for the first time in about nine months!

By the time my daughter came to the room to assist me, she was shocked to see what had just taken place, but I relayed to her how it all came about. She ran and called those that were around, who immediately came and I told them how it happened, how I heard God say to me, *"You can do it."* It was a day to be much remembered!

One Day, I Will Praise Like This!

Prior to this time, each time I watched the service at Faith Tabernacle on the Internet and saw people singing and praising God, I would say in my heart and sometimes audibly, "One day, not far from now, I will be praising God like this." Meanwhile, with the little strength I had, I made sure I praised Him. I would gather myself and praise God, sing and even dance, the best way I could.

Sometimes when the choir was ministering, I would take a bottle of water or a biro pen or whatever was around me, hold it like a microphone and say something such as: "Lord, one day and very, very soon, I will join these people in praising you this same way and even more. But in the mean time, this bottle of water is my microphone; I'm holding it to praise you today." I would keep shaking my body, confessing: "Nothing on earth will be able to take me away from the midst of these people. I'm a winner, indeed, and I shall keep on winning." I began to take aggressive faith steps!

Thereafter, virtually on a daily basis, I kept on receiving divine instructions on what to do. At the same time I kept on with my physical therapies, exercising different parts of my body. Not minding the pain, I kept at it.

One day, the Spirit of God said to me, *"You can climb the stair case again."* So I stood up, and began to attempt it. It was terribly difficult and painful the first time, but I kept at it. My son kept following me up as I tried this, just to take all possible caution. Today to the glory of God, I can do this with ease again. The devil has been put to shame!

Prior to this time, sleeping was an uphill task and even when I slept, I fought so hard in the sleep. When my children saw how I used to battle in the night, fighting spiritual battles in the night, rather than sleeping, one of them would come and anoint my head or sprinkle me with the blood of Jesus Christ.

Several times I woke up to find myself pleading the blood of Jesus Christ, or shouting the name of Jesus. My daughter, who used to sleep in my room, would be scared all through the night.

But suddenly, when the Lord turned my captivity and my turning point came, another evidence of it was that I began to sleep with ease. The night season was no longer a scary time. I would lie in bed, and be able to sleep! And even when I slept for just a few hours, I woke up refreshed. This was how things kept on turning and turning positively in my favour!

And then came the peak of it all, my son's graduation! It was a day never to be forgotten. The devil never wanted me to be alive to see that day. But to the glory of God and shame of the devil, I was physically present at the event! Before that time, I was only able to wear completely flat shoes but to put the devil to shame, I told him on my son's graduation day, I was going to put on my high-heeled shoes again and praise be to God, my heavenly Father made it possible.

On my son's graduation day, I was there, happy, strong, and excited! That was the first day I was able to sit for a number of hours without any terrible pain. I was present at the graduation and sat there all through, to the glory of God. Not only that, but for the first time in a long while, I was able to put on my high-heeled shoes again and ever since, I have worn them whenever I want to. Also, it was the first day in about ten months when I was able to climb the stairs of a two-storey building.

My son's graduation day was a day to be much remembered, a day I will never forget and a day of positive turnaround! From that very day, the pain started reducing dramatically. And today, to the glory of God, I'm totally pain-free, completely healed and made absolutely whole, to the glory of God. The God, who gave me my own turning point will also give you yours! It doesn't matter what you might be going through right now, put your faith in God - He turned my captivity; He will turn your own too!

Remember that the turning point came and then progressed gradually. It didn't come to an end just in one day; it was progressive. And even up untill now, things are progressively getting better for me, God will do the same thing for you. Don't lose hope! Don't give up! He is the same God; He will do yours too!

So, when I sayd "God opened my grave," it is a loaded statement. The good news is that the same God, who turned my captivity and opened my grave can do the same thing in your life. Therefore, never give up, and refuse to lose hope, because your future is bright.

The enemy thought that he had gotten his way in my life. But Halleluyah, the captivity-turning God turned my captivity and there and then, turned the table against my adversaries.

The God that we serve is a captivity-turning God. Indeed, He turned my captivity and now everything looks like a dream!

NOW, COMPLETELY RESCUED!

The scripture says:

For surely there is an end; and thine expectation shall not be cut off.

Proverbs 23:18

While the battle was on, it was as if I was going through a long, dark tunnel, to which there seemed to be no end. It was a long, tough and deadly battle, but an end to it finally came. Those ten months looked like ten years. But now, the battle is over!

However, even while in that condition, my confidence in God and His Word was totally unshaken concerning my total rescue. I knew, beyond every iota of doubt, that only He could get me out of that predicament, no one else but Him, and He did.

No matter what you may be going through in your life right now, know for sure that as long as you keep holding on to God, an end to it will surely come. Never lose hope! Don't give up!

Spiritually on Fire!

Now, much more than ever before, I am spiritually alert, active and sensitive. As soon as my turning point encounter started, I began my office work at home, as if I was in the office. My faith became activated; the symptoms not withstanding, less than two months after my return, by the special grace of God, two of the manuscripts I was working on were completed and published – two, not just one; just to slap the devil on both cheeks!

Halleluyah, oh! Oh, oh, oh, oh! I now have a renewed drive for the things of the Kingdom of God. It is like fire shut up in my bones, which no one can quench!

Mentally Alert!

Not only am I spiritually restored; I am no more mentally helpless! I can focus on the positive things of life now, more than ever before; in fact, I can safely say that my mind is now working at heaven's frequency. And one of the proofs is the books God enabled me to write; in fact, I have resumed going to the office in full force and carrying out all my official assignments. But that is jumping the gun - shortly, I will describe my home coming and how it went.

Physically Active!

To the glory of God, I am physically strong, normal, active and healthy again! The things I could not do previously, as a result of the attack, I can now do with ease. Sleeping is no problem at all, not to talk about driving, eating and many more such things. For a long time, I could not turn my neck, I wore neck braces just to help ease up the pain; but now, I can turn my neck to any direction! You will also recall that there was a lot of swelling of several parts of my body, like my feet, joints and so on. But to the glory of God, all the swellings are gone! I tell you, I am stronger now than I have ever been!

To show how physically active I have become since my return, I have gone on several mission trips with my husband within and outside the country. So, truly the devil lost out.

Emotionally Healthy

Now, I feel very balanced emotionally; I am not emotionally disturbed in any way, depressed or anxious. God has given me a new beginning; He has silenced all my mockers!

Indeed, a notable miracle has taken place in my life which cannot be denied by any. I am fully restored! As you read this, I see something positively notable happen in your life, as well.

> *The LORD is good, a strong hold in the day of trouble; and he knoweth them that trust in him.*
>
> *But with an overrunning flood he will make an utter end of the place thereof, and darkness shall pursue his enemies.*
>
> Nahum 1:7-8

9

HOME AT LAST!

There is truly nowhere like home! By this time, I had been away from home for many months and had missed home, church and fellowship, so naturally, I was eagerly looking forward to coming back home. And God did it! Eventually, I returned home victorious!

Upon my return, my husband sang this song of victory; and it has become a summary of my testimony.

I have seen the downfall of Satan
I have seen, seen the downfall of Satan
Glory be to God, glory be to Jesus
I have seen, seen the downfall of Satan
Glory be to God amen.

When I look at my right, I see Satan has fallen

When I look at my left, I see Satan has fallen

When I look at my front, I see Satan has fallen

When I look at my back, I see Satan has fallen

I have seen, seen... (refrain)

Reception at Light House

Upon my arrival, we went directly to our home – Light House. As we approached the gate, I remembered what Satan had whispered to me the night I was to travel, that the trip was going to be a journey of no return; I also recalled replying him with a song of victory, that God has promised and will never fail.

Truly it was the lie of the devil; he failed, he lost, he lied! Light House was filled with excited people - pastors, pastors' wives, relations, friends, neighbours and well-wishers.

They were all hilariously, energetically, excitedly, dedicatedly and joyfully ... praising God. We had a long session of high praises of the first order to God. I was quite overwhelmed to be a part of that praise time, to be back home, contrary to the scheming and lies of the devil and all his agents, and to see all those loving people once again.

Later At Mission Lodge (Our home in Canaan Land)

After the wonderful time at Light House, we went to Canaan Land later that day.

On arrival, we met another set of "God-praisers," ranging from Covenant University officials and students, to Pastors and wives, neighbours, friends, relations, well-wishers; the list is endless. We danced and jubilated at another glorious session of high praises and thanksgiving unto God. It was overwhelmingly glorious. There were presentations of songs, speeches and, so on. No one could celebrate enough, it seemed.

At the Faith Tabernacle, Canaan Land ... Wow!

Early in the morning of the next day, we drove gloriously to a special service at the Faith Tabernacle – the covenant home of Winners! I was so grateful to God to be physically back in the midst of Winners, contrary to the scheming of the devil.

I had watched services on the Internet while I was away and had told God that the devil could not take me away from the midst of these joyful people, and I strongly believed God to be back there in their midst, as soon as possible, God had made it a reality! I have every reason to be grateful to God. So, when I finally got back, the feeling I had was simply indescribable!

There was jubilation, shouts of praise and excitement in the congregation: as I entered the Church, tears flowed freely from some members of the congregation amidst shouting, dancing, clapping, jumping, you name it! It is better experienced than explained!

Then, suddenly, as I entered the sanctuary, I remembered that the last time I was here in church, I was wriggling in pain, feeling terribly weak, crying out to God for deliverance. But here was I filled with joy, smiles, strength and gratitude! Truly, He is a captivity turning God!

Personally, I was humbled to see such demonstration of love, and affection, primarily for God and for me; it was overwhelming and I was amazed at the faithfulness of God and the infallibility of His word. Many who heard about my triumphant return went to log on to the website of the church to watch the service, I later learnt.

Then, at the Covenant University

We then proceeded to the University Chapel in the evening, for another round of exciting, joyful, hearty, and hilarious praises to God. The service was dedicated to returning all glory to God Almighty, who stands to defend His Word always.

Here also, there were several presentations to God's glory.

Faith Academy and Kingdom Heritage

As if that was not enough, a time of praise and thanksgiving to God was held at both the Primary (Kingdom Heritage) and Secondary (Faith Academy) School arms of the Ministry. I was moved to tears, as the students sang such songs as, "The storm is over!" among others, and they also sang some original songs composed by the student, themselves.

To see such tender children singing touched me in no small way. They also recited poems such as "Welcome!" and many inspiring gymnastic displays, among several others, were rendered, just to give glory to God for His marvelous acts. It was delightfully surprising!

Visits from individuals and groups

Several individuals and groups paid visits from within and outside the country. I could not help but observe how several people, both from within our ministry network and from other ministries, trooped in to rejoice with us; and those visits continued for months after my arrival. Even as I write this material , people are still visiting.

Everyone came to rejoice with us and to give all the glory back to God alone, to whom it is due. I was pleasantly surprised and humbled by all the display of love and I must say that I felt the depth of the warmth and affection of so many people.

To all such, I say thank you, I am grateful and may the Lord reward you!

My testimony has become like that of Sarah:

> *... God hath made me to laugh, so that all that hear will laugh with me.*
>
> Genesis 21:6

And Finally ...!

An end came to all the malicious publications! All my mockers were put to shame, or, as my husband says, 'shamified!'

Truly, God has delivered my soul from death (Ps. 56:13). Against the wishes of my enemies, He

> *...turned for me my mourning into dancing: thou hast put off my sackcloth and girded me with gladness.*
>
> Psalms 30:11

He clothed my enemies with shame!

With a heart full of gratitude to God, I join the Psalm-ist and say,

I will praise thee for ever, because thou hast done it .
                                                    Psalms 52:9a

God

... delivered my soul from death, mine eyes from tears and my feet from falling.
                                                    Psalms 116:8

And He brought me out of darkness and the shadow of death, broke my bands asunder... and broke the gates of brass and cut the bars of iron in sunder.
                                                Psalms 107:14, 16

I know, beyond every iota of doubt, that I overcame this ordeal for a reason – to carry out a specific divine mandate. I sure will live the rest of my life for Him, to His glory and to fulfill His divine mandate. Assuredly, God has worked an undeniable miracle in my life. I literarily walked through the valley of the shadow of death, but I emerged victorious and fully restored to the glory of God!

God is no respecter of persons. No matter the situation you are in today, never mistake it for your portion. Keep your hope in God alive. Believe what the Word of God says about you and, you will surely become it. Hold on to God and he will turn your ridicule to miracle, and your shame to fame. I can tell you this because He has done it in my life!

So, I boldly declare,

God is too faithful to fail!

He is dependable!

He is more than enough!

Therefore,

There is no closed case with God.

He opened my grave and He can open yours too!

VALUABLE LIFE
LESSONS

And we know that all things work together for good to them that love God, to them who are the called according to his purpose.

Romans 8:28

Robert Schuller once said, "Tough times never last, but tough people do." That presupposes that tough times are real, but the good news is that no matter how real your tough times may be, God is going to turn your adversity into victory and your setback into stepping-stones!

Please never make the mistake of assuming that tough times are from God, no, He is not the author of them; they are not from Him. However, in the midst of those tough situations, God can take advantage of them and turn things around for your good, as was the case with me. This is why the word of God says:

all things work together for good to them that love God
Romans 8:28

The devil wanted to destroy my life, but God did not only rescue me, He also taught me several lessons that now have a great effect on my perception of life and Christianity. Below are a few of them.

Intimacy with God!

The first and most significant lesson I learnt, as I walked through the valley of the shadow of death, was intimacy with God. When tough times knock on your door, don't run away from God; run towards Him; never allow anything separate you form God, because it is to Him you will return at the end of your earthly journey.

Who shall separate us from the love of Christ? shall tribulation, or distress, or persecution, or famine, or nakedness, or peril, or sword?

Nay, in all these things we are more than conquerors through him that loved us.

Romans 8:35,37

My husband often says that whatever God cannot do may it remain undone; in other words, he acknowledges God as the only source of true and lasting help!

Secondly, I learnt that no matter how intense the pressure of the problem, I must choose to focus on God and not the problem (James 4:8). When you focus on God, you will be moved to obey Him, even when you can't immediately see the benefits.

Consciously Think Thoughts of Victory.

Your life will always move in the direction of your dominant thought. In other words, your life will follow your thoughts; that is why the Bible says,

> *For as he thinketh in his heart, so is he: Eat and drink, saith he to thee; but his heart is not with thee.*
> Proverbs 23:7

You must guard your mind earnestly during tough times; focus on the positive things of life in your thoughts. And in case you are being barraged by negative thoughts, don't fight them with positive thoughts; fight them with positive words! Seek to see the right part of life in every situation.

Remember, your thinking defines your living!

Expect to Come Out Victorious

Naturally, when faced with difficult and challenging

situations in life, you feel as though you will never come out of it. But that is a lie of the devil because you will not only come out, you will do so triumphantly! The key is – don't expect to stay there; instead, expect to come out of it, victorious.

Your expectation sets a pace for your experience. That is why Bishop David Oyedepo says, "What you don't expect, you never experience." Please believe that God has paid for all the good things you need in life, but you only take delivery of them by your strong expectations. So expect victory and it will be yours. I see you triumph over the works of the enemy, in Jesus' name.

... thy expectation shall not be cut off.
Proverbs 24:14b

Build, Value and Enjoy Profitable Relationships

Man is created to connect; in other words, no man was created to function as an island. You need relationship with people to triumph over life's situations. There are certain battles you cannot fight alone; certain races you cannot run alone and expect to win; your strength, therefore, is in the quality of person to whom you are connected.

Relationship is simply defined as connection between

two or more people. Haven't you heard?

> *And if one prevail against him, two shall withstand him; and a threefold cord is not quickly broken.*
>
> Ecclesiastes 4:12

Friend, you know the saying, "united we stand, divided we fall," so, value people. You need them. You only attract what you value. To enjoy such relationships, therefore, conscious steps need be taken to build them. They won't just happen on their own.

> *A man that hath friends must shew himself friendly: and there is a friend that sticketh closer than a brother.*
>
> Proverbs 18:24

In relationships, you have basically three levels: a higher level, which involves relating profitably with your superiors or mentors, so you can draw from them; same level relationship with your peers, so you can share with them and lower level relationships, so you can reach out to them. You have a responsibility to build, value and nurture those profitable relationships before you can enjoy them.

> *... but woe to him that is alone when he falleth; for he hath not another to help him up.*
>
> Ecclesiastes 4:10b

I employed all the above during the period of my attack and they worked for me, they will work for you too.

Seek and Receive Necessary Counsel

Proverbs 24:6 says:

> *For by wise counsel thou shalt make thy war: and in multitude of counsellors there is safety.*

Counsel is an integral part of life. There are people who are more knowledgeable than you are in several aspects of life. Especially in times of challenges, wisdom demands that you seek out for such people and tap into their wealth of knowledge. A wise man once said: "If I have seen any further, it is by standing on the shoulders of those who have gone ahead." One major way you can stand on the shoulders of those who have gone ahead is through counseling.

There will always be people who are in a position to give you godly, spiritual and professional counsel on various issues of life.

There will always be people who know better than you do. Locate them and draw from them.

However, this must be done with great caution. You have a responsibility to ensure that whomever you ask counsel from, does not, in the process, cancel your destiny. You must employ the weapon of wisdom in locating right counselors.

Cultivate a Gratitude Attitude

Admittedly, a gratitude attitude is not naturally easy

during times of great difficulty, but cultivating one is a sure way of securing the help of God for your release from the predicaments of life. When I am talking about gratitude, I mean towards God and to man.

Learn to be appreciative. Be grateful to God for whom He has made you into and for His faithfulness; be grateful to men, especially people around you. Appreciate their help and kindness to you – never take such for granted.

The natural man wants to complain, murmur and grumble, especially in difficult times. No matter how tight the situation may appear, resist the temptation to murmur or grumble. Remember that those who murmured in Bible days were destroyed by the destroyer (1 Cor. 10:10). Rather, be thankful!

"To be thankful is to be 'tankful'" – Bishop Oyedepo

The Healing Power of Foods

God has made provision for sound health for man, and this great healing power is locked up in the common foods you may be taking for granted. Learn to eat right. I have come to discover, more than ever, that eating sensibly enhances healthy living. One great key I have discovered is to "juice my vegetables and eat my fruits."

I have also learnt to let my food be my medicine and my medicine be my food.

All these principles are additional keys to the ones earlier mentioned in this book. Don't just read them, but apply them, and tomorrow, men will gather to share your testimony!

RESCUE SCRIPTURES

My son, attend to my words; incline thine ear unto my sayings.

Let them not depart from thine eyes; keep them in the midst of thine heart.

For they are life unto those that find them, and health to all their flesh.

Proverbs 4:20-22

The Word of God is my only source of life. I have absolute confidence in its infallibility; it was one of the most important things that helped me during my time of crisis. I value and have great respect for the Word of God; I used to confess scriptures daily.

There are many specific scriptures that God gave me

during that time. I had them written down and some of them were boldly written and pasted in strategic places around the house, especially, in my room. I cannot list them all, but I will attempt to list some of them here.

You do not have to be in a life-threatening situation to use God's Word. The Word is meant to be part and parcel of our daily life. So, I strongly believe that these scriptures will be tremendously helpful to you in life. You can use them, also, as part of your daily confession. I still use them, even today.

These scriptures can even be used as a reference material in your journey of life. I guarantee you of their infallibility. The Word of God works –always! So, don't just read these scriptures once; but read them over and again, so that the benefits they carry can be delivered to your life. **Only what you discover in the Word will be delivered to you in this world.**

So, come along with me, as we travel through these life-giving scriptures. Open your heart as you carefully go through them for a definite encounter that you will live to remember all your life.

Let's get started!

1.   Exodus 23:25

And ye shall serve the LORD your God, and he shall bless thy bread, and thy water; and I will take sickness away from the midst of thee.

2.   Deuteronomy 7:15

And the LORD will take away from thee all sickness,

3.   Deuteronomy 30:19

... I have set before you life and death, blessing and cursing: therefore choose life, that both thou and thy seed may live.

4.   Joshua 21:45

There failed not ought of any good thing which the LORD had spoken unto the house of Israel; all came to pass.

5.   1 Chronicles 16: 21-22

He suffered no man to do them wrong: yea, he reproved kings for their sakes, Saying, Touch not mine anointed, and do my prophets no harm.

6.   2 Chronicles 30:20

And the LORD hearkened to Hezekiah, and healed the people.

7.   Nehemiah 8:10

... for the joy of the LORD is your strength.

8.   Job 5:12

He disappointeth the devices of the crafty, so that their hands cannot perform their enterprise.

9.   Job 42:10

And the LORD turned the captivity of Job, when he prayed for his friends: also the LORD gave Job twice as much as he had before.

10.   Psalms 3:5

I laid me down and slept; I awaked; for the LORD sustained me.

11.   Psalms 4:8

I will both lay me down in peace, and sleep: for thou, LORD, only makest me dwell in safety.

12.   Psalms 23: 1;6

The LORD is my shepherd; I shall not want.

Surely goodness and mercy shall follow me all the days of my life: and I will dwell in the house of the LORD for ever.

13.   Psalms 30:1-2

I will extol thee, O LORD; for thou hast lifted me up, and hast not made my foes to rejoice over me.

O LORD my God, I cried unto thee, and thou hast healed me.

14.   Psalms 30:11

Thou hast turned for me my mourning into dancing: thou

hast put off my sackcloth, and girded me with gladness;

15. Psalms 34:5

They looked unto him, and were lightened: and their faces were not ashamed.

16. Psalms 34:10

The young lions do lack, and suffer hunger: but they that seek the LORD shall not want any good thing.

17. Psalms 34:7

The angel of the LORD encampeth round about them that fear him, and delivereth them.

18. Psalms 46: 1

God is our refuge and strength, a very present help in trouble.

19. Psalms 60:11

Give us help from trouble: for vain is the help of man.

20. Psalms 71:21

Thou shalt increase my greatness, and comfort me on every side.

21. Psalms 84:11

For the LORD God is a sun and shield: the LORD will give grace and glory: no good thing will he withhold from them that walk uprightly.

22. Psalms 89:22-23

The enemy shall not exact upon him; nor the son of wickedness afflict him.

And I will beat down his foes before his face, and plague them that hate him.

23. Psalms 89:34

My covenant will I not break, nor alter the thing that is gone out of my lips.

24. Psalms 91: 1; 10; 15-16

He that dwelleth in the secret place of the most High shall abide under the shadow of the Almighty.

There shall no evil befall thee, neither shall any plague come nigh thy dwelling.

He shall call upon me, and I will answer him: I will be with him in trouble; I will deliver him, and honour him.

With long life will I satisfy him, and shew him my salvation.

25. Psalms 94:1

LORD God, to whom vengeance belongeth; O God, to whom vengeance belongeth, shew thyself.

26. Psalm 103:3-5

Who forgiveth all thine iniquities; who healeth all

thy diseases;

Who redeemeth thy life from destruction; who crowneth thee with lovingkindness and tender mercies;

Who satisfieth thy mouth with good things; so that thy youth is renewed like the eagle's.

27.   Psalm 107:20

He sent his word, and healed them, and delivered them from their destructions.

28.   Psalm 118:17

I shall not die, but live, and declare the works of the LORD.

29.   Proverbs 4:20-23

My son, attend to my words; incline thine ear unto my sayings.

Let them not depart from thine eyes; keep them in the midst of thine heart.

For they are life unto those that find them, and health to all their flesh.

Keep thy heart with all diligence; for out of it are the issues of life.

30.   Proverbs 18:10

The name of the LORD is a strong tower: the righteous runneth into it, and is safe.

31.   Provrebs 23:18

For surely there is an end; and thine expectation shall not be cut off.

32.   Proverbs 30:5

Every word of God is pure: he is a shield unto them that put their trust in him.

33.   Ecclesiastes 9:4

For to him that is joined to all the living there is hope: for a living dog is better than a dead lion.

34.   Isaiah 3:10

Say ye to the righteous, that it shall be well with him.

35.   Isaiah 12:3

Therefore with joy shall ye draw water out of the wells of salvation.

36.   Isaiah 41:10-13

Fear thou not; for I am with thee: be not dismayed; for I am thy God: I will strengthen thee; yea, I will help thee; yea, I will uphold thee with the right hand of my righteousness.

Behold, all they that were incensed against thee shall be ashamed and confounded: they shall be as nothing; and they that strive with thee shall perish.

Thou shalt seek them, and shalt not find them, even them that contended with thee: they that war against thee shall be as nothing, and as a thing of nought.

For I the LORD thy God will hold thy right hand, saying unto thee, Fear not; I will help thee.

37. Isaiah 43:2

When thou passest through the waters, I will be with thee; and through the rivers, they shall not overflow thee: when thou walkest through the fire, thou shalt not be burned; neither shall the flame kindle upon thee.

38. Isaiah 43:18-19; 26

Remember ye not the former things, neither consider the things of old.

Behold, I will do a new thing; now it shall spring forth; shall ye not know it? I will even make a way in the wilderness, and rivers in the desert.

Put me in remembrance: let us plead together: declare thou, that thou mayest be justified.

39. Isaiah 44:3, 24-27

For I will pour water upon him that is thirsty, and floods upon the dry ground: I will pour my spirit upon thy seed, and my blessing upon thine offspring:

Thus saith the LORD, thy redeemer, and he that formed thee from the womb, I am the LORD that maketh all things;

That frustrateth the tokens of the liars, and maketh diviners mad; that turneth wise men backward, and maketh their knowledge foolish;

That confirmeth the word of his servant, and performeth the counsel of his messengers; that saith to Jerusalem, Thou shalt be inhabited; and to the cities of Judah, Ye shall be built, and I will raise up the decayed places thereof:

That saith to the deep, Be dry, and I will dry up thy rivers:

40.   Isaiah 49:25

But thus saith the LORD, Even the captives of the mighty shall be taken away, and the prey of the terrible shall be delivered: for I will contend with him that contendeth with thee, and I will save thy children.

41.   Isaiah 53:1, 5

Who hath believed our report? and to whom is the arm of the LORD revealed?

But he was wounded for our transgressions, he was bruised for our iniquities: the chastisement of our peace was upon him; and with his stripes we are healed.

42.   Isaiah 54:14-15,17

In righteousness shalt thou be established: thou shalt be far from oppression; for thou shalt not fear: and from terror; for it shall not come near thee.

Behold, they shall surely gather together, but not by me: whosoever shall gather together against thee shall fall for thy sake.

No weapon that is formed against thee shall prosper; and every tongue that shall rise against thee in judgment thou shalt condemn. This is the heritage of the servants of the LORD, and their righteousness is of me, saith the LORD.

43. Isaiah 59:19

...When the enemy shall come in like a flood, the Spirit of the LORD shall lift up a standard against him.

44. Jeremiah 8:22

Is there no balm in Gilead; is there no physician there? why then is not the health of the daughter of my people recovered?

45. Jeremiah 29:11

For I know the thoughts that I think toward you, saith the LORD, thoughts of peace, and not of evil, to give you an expected end.

46. Jeremiah 30:16-17

Therefore all they that devour thee shall be devoured; and all thine adversaries, every one of them, shall go into captivity; and they that spoil thee shall be a spoil, and all that prey upon thee will I give for a prey.

For I will restore health unto thee, and I will heal

thee of thy wounds, saith the LORD; because they called thee an Outcast, saying, This is Zion, whom no man seeketh after.

47. Jeremiah 32:27

Behold, I am the LORD, the God of all flesh: is there any thing too hard for me?

48. Jeremiah 33:3

Call unto me, and I will answer thee, and shew thee great and mighty things, which thou knowest not.

49. Ezekiel 37:3, 7

And he said unto me, Son of man, can these bones live? And I answered, O Lord GOD, thou knowest.

So I prophesied as I was commanded: and as I prophesied, there was a noise, and behold a shaking, and the bones came together, bone to his bone.

50. Daniel 11:32b

... but the people that do know their God shall be strong, and do exploits

51. Hosea 12:13

And by a prophet the LORD brought Israel out of Egypt, and by a prophet was he preserved.

52. Hosea 13:14

I will ransom them from the power of the grave; I

will redeem them from death: O death, I will be thy plagues; O grave, I will be thy destruction: repentance shall be hid from mine eyes.

53. Joel 2:27

And ye shall know that I am in the midst of Israel, and that I am the LORD your God, and none else: and my people shall never be ashamed.

54. Joel 2:32

And it shall come to pass, that whosoever shall call on the name of the LORD shall be delivered ...

55. Joel 3:10b

... Let the weak say, I am strong

56. Obadiah 17

But upon mount Zion shall be deliverance, and there shall be holiness; and the house of Jacob shall possess their possessions.

57. Jonah 2:2

And said, I cried by reason of mine affliction unto the LORD, and he heard me; out of the belly of hell cried I, and thou heardest my voice.

58. Nahum 1:9

He will make an utter end: affliction shall not rise up the second time.

59. Habakkuk 2:4

... but the just shall live by his faith

60. Habakkuk 3:18 -19

Yet I will rejoice in the LORD, I will joy in the God of my salvation.

The LORD God is my strength,

61. Zephaniah 3:19-20

Behold, at that time I will undo all that afflict thee: and I will save her that halteth, and gather her that was driven out;

At that time will I bring you again, even in the time that I gather you: for I will make you a name and a praise among all people of the earth, when I turn back your captivity before your eyes, saith the LORD.

62. Zechariah 9:11-12

As for thee also, by the blood of thy covenant I have sent forth thy prisoners out of the pit wherein is no water.

Turn you to the strong hold, ye prisoners of hope: even to day do I declare that I will render double unto thee;

63. Malachi 3:6, 17

For I am the LORD, I change not; therefore ye sons of Jacob are not consumed

And they shall be mine, saith the LORD of hosts, in

that day when I make up my jewels; and I will spare them, as a man spareth his own son that serveth him.

64.   Malachi 4:2-3

But unto you that fear my name shall the Sun of righteousness arise with healing in his wings; and ye shall go forth, and grow up as calves of the stall.

And ye shall tread down the wicked; for they shall be ashes under the soles of your feet in the day that I shall do this, saith the LORD of hosts.

65.   Matthew 8:2b-3, 13, 17b

... Lord, if thou wilt, thou canst make me clean. And Jesus put forth his hand, and touched him, saying, I will; be thou clean. And immediately his leprosy was cleansed.

And Jesus said unto the centurion, Go thy way; and as thou hast believed, so be it done unto thee. And his servant was healed in the selfsame hour.

... Himself took our infirmities, and bare our sicknesses.

66.   Matthew 9:20-23

And, behold, a woman, which was diseased with an issue of blood twelve years, came behind him, and touched the hem of his garment:

For she said within herself, If I may but touch his garment, I shall be whole.

But Jesus turned him about, and when he saw her, he said, Daughter, be of good comfort; thy faith hath made thee whole. And the woman was made whole from that hour.

67. Matthew 11:28, 30

Come unto me, all ye that labour and are heavy laden, and I will give you rest.

For my yoke is easy, and my burden is light.

68. Matthew 15:13

But he answered and said, Every plant, which my heavenly Father hath not planted, shall be rooted up.

69. Matthew 17:20-21

... If ye have faith as a grain of mustard seed, ye shall say unto this mountain, Remove hence to yonder place; and it shall remove; and nothing shall be impossible unto you.

Howbeit this kind goeth not out but by prayer and fasting.

70. Matthew 18:18-19

Verily I say unto you, Whatsoever ye shall bind on earth shall be bound in heaven: and whatsoever ye shall loose on earth shall be loosed in heaven.

Again I say unto you, That if two of you shall agree on earth as touching any thing that they shall ask, it shall be done for them of my Father which is in heaven.

71. Matthew 21:22

And all things, whatsoever ye shall ask in prayer, believing, ye shall receive.

72. Mark 1:41-42

And Jesus, moved with compassion, put forth his hand, and touched him, and saith unto him, I will; be thou clean.

73. Mark 7:27

But Jesus said unto her, Let the children first be filled: for it is not meet to take the children's bread, and to cast it unto the dogs.

74. Mark 9:23

Jesus said unto him, If thou canst believe, all things are possible to him that believeth.

75. Mark 10:27

And Jesus looking upon them saith, With men it is impossible, but not with God: for with God all things are possible.

76. Mark 11:22-23

And Jesus answering saith unto them, Have faith in God.

For verily I say unto you, That whosoever shall say unto this mountain, Be thou removed, and be thou cast into the sea; and shall not doubt in his heart, but shall believe that those things which he saith shall come to pass; he shall have whatsoever he saith.

77. Mark 16:17-18

And these signs shall follow them that believe; In my name shall they cast out devils; they shall speak with new tongues;

They shall take up serpents; and if they drink any deadly thing, it shall not hurt them; they shall lay hands on the sick, and they shall recover.

78. Luke 1:45

And blessed is she that believed: for there shall be a performance of those things which were told her from the Lord.

79. Luke 11:9-10

And I say unto you, Ask, and it shall be given you; seek, and ye shall find; knock, and it shall be opened unto you.

For every one that asketh receiveth; and he that seeketh findeth; and to him that knocketh it shall be opened.

80. Luke 13:11-13

And, behold, there was a woman which had a spirit of infirmity eighteen years, and was bowed together, and could in no wise lift up herself.

And when Jesus saw her, he called her to him, and said unto her, Woman, thou art loosed from thine infirmity.

And he laid his hands on her: and immediately she was made straight, and glorified God.

81. Luke 18:5

And shall not God avenge his own elect, which cry day and night unto him, though he bear long with them?

82. Luke 21:13, 15

And it shall turn to you for a testimony.

For I will give you a mouth and wisdom, which all your adversaries shall not be able to gainsay nor resist.

83. John 1:5

And the light shineth in darkness; and the darkness comprehended it not.

84. John 4:50

Jesus saith unto him, Go thy way; thy son liveth. And the man believed the word that Jesus had spoken unto him, and he went his way.

85. John 6:63

It is the spirit that quickeneth; the flesh profiteth

nothing: the words that I speak unto you, they are spirit, and they are life.

86. John 8:32

And ye shall know the truth, and the truth shall make you free.

87. John 8:36

If the Son therefore shall make you free, ye shall be free indeed.

88. John 10:10

The thief cometh not, but for to steal, and to kill, and to destroy: I am come that they might have life, and that they might have it more abundantly.

89. John 14:13

And whatsoever ye shall ask in my name, that will I do, that the Father may be glorified in the Son.

90. John 16:23

And in that day ye shall ask me nothing. Verily, verily, I say unto you, Whatsoever ye shall ask the Father in my name, he will give it you.

91. Acts 2:21

And it shall come to pass, that whosoever shall call on the name of the Lord shall be saved.

92. Acts 4:12

Neither is there salvation in any other: for there is none other name under heaven given among men, whereby we must be saved

93. Acts 9:34

And Peter said unto him, Aeneas, Jesus Christ maketh thee whole: arise, and make thy bed. And he arose immediately.

94. Acts 19:11-12

And God wrought special miracles by the hands of Paul:

So that from his body were brought unto the sick handkerchiefs or aprons, and the diseases departed from them, and the evil spirits went out of them.

95. Acts 27:34

Wherefore I pray you to take some meat: for this is for your health: for there shall not an hair fall from the head of any of you.

96. Acts 10:34

Then Peter opened his mouth, and said, Of a truth I perceive that God is no respecter of persons.

97. Acts 10:38

How God anointed Jesus of Nazareth with the Holy

Ghost and with power: who went about doing good, and healing all that were oppressed of the devil; for God was with him.

98.   Romans 8:11, 31-32, 35

But if the Spirit of him that raised up Jesus from the dead dwell in you, he that raised up Christ from the dead shall also quicken your mortal bodies by his Spirit that dwelleth in you.

What shall we then say to these things? If God be for us, who can be against us?

He that spared not his own Son, but delivered him up for us all, how shall he not with him also freely give us all things?

Who shall separate us from the love of Christ? shall tribulation, or distress, or persecution, or famine, or nakedness, or peril, or sword?

99.   Romans 9:15-16

... I will have mercy on whom I will have mercy, and I will have compassion on whom I will have compassion.

So then it is not of him that willeth, nor of him that runneth, but of God that sheweth mercy.

100. 1 Corinthians 6:20; 7:1

For ye are bought with a price: therefore glorify God in your body, and in your spirit, which are God's.

101. 2 Corinthians 6:2

For he saith, I have heard thee in a time accepted, and in the day of salvation have I succoured thee: behold, now is the accepted time; behold, now is the day of salvation.

102. 2 Corinthians 10:3-5

For though we walk in the flesh, we do not war after the flesh:

For the weapons of our warfare are not carnal, but mighty through God to the pulling down of strong holds;

Casting down imaginations, and every high thing that exalteth itself against the knowledge of God, and bringing into captivity every thought to the obedience of Christ.

103. 2 Corinthians 12:9a

And he said unto me, My grace is sufficient for thee: for my strength is made perfect in weakness.

104. Galatians 3:13

Christ hath redeemed us from the curse of the law, being made a curse for us: for it is written, Cursed is every one that hangeth on a tree.

105. Galatians 6:17

From henceforth let no man trouble me: for I bear in

my body the marks of the Lord Jesus.

106. Ephesians 2:6

And hath raised us up together, and made us sit together in heavenly places in Christ Jesus:

107. Ephesians 6:10-13

Finally, my brethren, be strong in the Lord, and in the power of his might.

Put on the whole armour of God, that ye may be able to stand against the wiles of the devil.

For we wrestle not against flesh and blood, but against principalities, against powers, against the rulers of the darkness of this world, against spiritual wickedness in high places.

Wherefore take unto you the whole armour of God, that ye may be able to withstand in the evil day, and having done all, to stand.

Stand therefore, having your loins girt about with truth, and having on the breastplate of righteousness;

108. Philippians 1:6

Being confident of this very thing, that he which hath begun a good work in you will perform it until the day of Jesus Christ.

109. Philippians 1:28

And in nothing terrified by your adversaries: which

is to them an evident token of perdition, but to you of salvation, and that of God.

110. Phil 2:10-11

That at the name of Jesus every knee should bow, of things in heaven, and things in earth, and things under the earth;

And that every tongue should confess that Jesus Christ is Lord, to the glory of God the Father.

111. Philippians 4:6-7

Be careful for nothing; but in every thing by prayer and supplication with thanksgiving let your requests be made known unto God.

And the peace of God, which passeth all understanding, shall keep your hearts and minds through Christ Jesus.

112. Colossians 1:12-13

Giving thanks unto the Father, which hath made us meet to be partakers of the inheritance of the saints in light:

Who hath delivered us from the power of darkness, and hath translated us into the kingdom of his dear Son.

113. Colossians 2:10

And ye are complete in him, which is the head of

all principality and power:

114. 1 Thessalonians 5:16, 18, 23-24

Rejoice evermore.

In every thing give thanks: for this is the will of God in Christ Jesus concerning you.

And the very God of peace sanctify you wholly; and I pray God your whole spirit and soul and body be preserved blameless unto the coming of our Lord Jesus Christ.

Faithful is he that calleth you, who also will do it.

115. 2 Thessalonians 1:6

Seeing it is a righteous thing with God to recompense tribulation to them that trouble you.

116. 2 Thessalonians 3:3

But the Lord is faithful, who shall stablish you, and keep you from evil.

117. 2 Timothy 1:7; 18

For God hath not given us the spirit of fear; but of power, and of love, and of a sound mind.

This charge I commit unto thee, son Timothy, according to the prophecies which went before on thee, that thou by them mightest war a good warfare.

118. 1 Timothy 2:6

Who gave himself a ransom for all, to be testified in due time.

119. 1 Timothy 6:12

Fight the good fight of faith, lay hold on eternal life, whereunto thou art also called, and hast professed a good profession before many witnesses.

120. 2 Timothy 3:11

Persecutions, afflictions, which came unto me ...but out of them all the Lord delivered me.

121. Titus 2:11

For the grace of God that bringeth salvation hath appeared to all men.

122. Hebrews 1:3

Who being the brightness of his glory, and the express image of his person, and upholding all things by the word of his power, when he had by himself purged our sins, sat down on the right hand of the Majesty on high.

123. Hebrews 4:12, 15-16

For the word of God is quick, and powerful, and sharper than any twoedged sword, piercing even to the dividing asunder of soul and spirit, and of the joints and marrow, and is a discerner of the thoughts and intents of the heart.

For we have not an high priest which cannot be touched with the feeling of our infirmities; but was in all points tempted like as we are, yet without sin.

Let us therefore come boldly unto the throne of grace, that we may obtain mercy, and find grace to help in time of need.

124. Hebrews 10:23

Let us hold fast the profession of our faith without wavering; (for he is faithful that promised).

125. Hebrews 11:1-2

Now faith is the substance of things hoped for, the evidence of things not seen.

For by it the elders obtained a good report.

126. Hebrews 12:29

For our God is a consuming fire.

127. Hebrews 13:8

Jesus Christ the same yesterday, and to day, and for ever.

128. James 5:13-16

Is any among you afflicted? let him pray. Is any merry? let him sing psalms.

Is any sick among you? let him call for the elders of the church; and let them pray over him, anointing him with oil in the name of the Lord:

And the prayer of faith shall save the sick, and the Lord shall raise him up; and if he have committed sins, they shall be forgiven him.

Confess your faults one to another, and pray one for another, that ye may be healed. The effectual fervent prayer of a righteous man availeth much.

129. 1 Peter 2:24b

... by whose stripes ye were healed.

130. 1 Peter 5:7

Casting all your care upon him; for he careth for you.

131. 2 Peter 1:3-4

According as his divine power hath given unto us all things that pertain unto life and godliness, through the knowledge of him that hath called us to glory and virtue:

Whereby are given unto us exceeding great and precious promises: that by these ye might be partakers of the divine nature, having escaped the corruption that is in the world through lust.

132. 1 John 1:5

This then is the message which we have heard of

him, and declare unto you, that God is light, and in him is no darkness at all.

133. 1 John 5:4

For whatsoever is born of God overcometh the world: and this is the victory that overcometh the world, even our faith.

134. 1 John 3:8b

For this purpose the Son of God was manifested, that he might destroy the works of the devil

135. 1 John 5:14

And this is the confidence that we have in him, that, if we ask any thing according to his will, he heareth us.

136. 1 John 5:15

And if we know that he hear us, whatsoever we ask, we know that we have the petitions that we desired of him.

137. Revelation 5:5

And one of the elders saith unto me, Weep not: behold, the Lion of the tribe of Juda, the Root of David, hath prevailed to open the book, and to loose the seven seals thereof.

138. Revelation 12:11

And they overcame him by the blood of the Lamb,

and by the word of their testimony; and they loved not their lives unto the death.

139. Revelation 22:1-2

And he shewed me a pure river of water of life, clear as crystal, proceeding out of the throne of God and of the Lamb.

In the midst of the street of it, and on either side of the river, was there the tree of life, which bare twelve manner of fruits, and yielded her fruit every month: and the leaves of the tree were for the healing of the nations.

140. Revelation 22:13

I am Alpha and Omega, the beginning and the end, the first and the last.

RESCUE PRAYER

As this book comes to an end, I feel a tremendous urgency in my spirit to pray a rescue prayer for you. But before this, I want to ask you a question; have you ever consciously asked Jesus Christ to come into your heart? Are you born again? If you have never given your life to Jesus Christ, you need to be born-again. Divine rescue is the heritage of only those that are saved.

The Word of God says in Romans 10:9-10:

That if thou shalt confess with thy mouth the Lord Jesus, and shalt believe in thine heart that God hath raised him from the dead, thou shalt be saved.

For with the heart man believeth unto righteousness; and with the mouth confession is made unto salvation.

You need to repent of your sins, confess Jesus as your Savior and give Him the lordship of your life. Your life shall never be the same. So, pray this prayer along with me right now:

Jesus Christ, I come to You today. I am a sinner and cannot help myself. I ask You right now to please forgive my sins and make me clean with Your blood. I sincerely ask You to deliver me from Satan's power and accept me as Your very own child. I will serve You as long as I live. I therefore accept You as my Savior, Lord and Deliverer right now. Thank You for saving me. Now I know I am born again and a child of God, in Jesus' name!

If you prayed that prayer, you are now born again and can then lay hold on your inheritance in Christ, which includes divine rescue.

Open your heart for divine intervention in your affairs, as we pray right now:

Prayer

Father, I come to You right now, in the name of Jesus Christ, on behalf of this person reading this book, who desires rescue or divine intervention in any area of life.

Lord God Almighty, there is no distance problem with you. So, wherever this individual might be right now, I ask You to move on the scene to supernaturally deliver and set this person free. Take over the battle of his/her life right now and wrought deliverance.

In the mighty name of Jesus Christ, Satan, I rebuke you and frustrate your activities in the life of this individual right now! Take off your hands! Your plan of destruction for this person's life, as it relates to his/her joy, peace, fulfillment, marriage, finances, health, job and every other area of life is, hereby, frustrated in Jesus name. Loose this individual completely right now, from the crown of his/her head to the sole of his/her feet!

By the power in the mighty name of Jesus, I speak to your life; I curse every torment, disease, sickness, affliction, difficulty, crisis and every evil of Satan in your life. I curse every form of darkness around your life and I command light to come into you, in Jesus' name.

I speak freedom, liberty, wholeness, health, strength, joy, peace, and blessings into your life in Jesus' name. You shall no longer be robbed of your inheritance in Christ. Henceforth, your life shall be a living proof of the faithfulness of God Almighty, in Jesus' name!

Father, I thank You for confirming this prayer in the life of this person. Thank You for testimonies that are coming forth, as a result of answers to this prayer. Thank you, Lord, in Jesus' Name. Amen!

ABOUT THE AUTHOR

FAITH ABIOLA OYEDEPO has brought hope, joy and life into many homes in her generation.

Having received a ministry for building godly homes, she has dedicated her life to showing people God's perfect will for their homes, and helping to lead them back there. Her weekly newspaper column, Family Matters, has helped, in no small way, in achieving this goal.

She has shown in practical terms, and through deep spiritual insight that the home can be the Eden God created it to be.

Pastor Faith has written more than 10 books, including: Marriage Covenant, Making Marriage Work and Raising Godly Children.

An anointed preacher of the gospel, Pastor Faith Oyedepo has been doggedly supportive of her husband (Bishop David Oyedepo) in the undaunting work of the ministry. She has four children — David Jnr., Isaac, Love and Joys.

Other Books by Faith A. Oyedepo

Making Marriage Work

Marriage Covenant

Raising Godly Children

You Can Overcome Anxiety

The Dignity Of The Believer

A Living Witness

Communion Table

Nurturing The Incorruptible Seed

Service: The Master Key

Stirring Up The Grace Of God

Building A Successful Family

The Spirit of Faith

Visit our website for weekly articles
by the author:
http://www.davidoyedepoministries.org